Put Right Something That's Wrong

Albert Nolan OP

Put Right Something That's Wrong

The Call to Action, Education, Justice, *Kairos*, and Leadership

Albert Nolan OP

Adelaide
2023

Text copyright ©2023 remains the individual authors and ATF Press for the collection. All rights reserved. Except for any fair dealing under the Copyright Act, no part of the publication may be reproduced by any means without prior permission. Inquiries should be made in the first instance with the publisher.

Photo on front cover is of Albert Nolan and was taken around 1983 in South Africa. Copyright Vice-Province of Southern Africa. Used with permission.

Cover Design: Myf Cadwallader

Cardijn Studies: On the Church in the World of Today
Volume 4, Number 2, 2023

The *Cardijn Studies* journal is a refereed journal which aims to document the history of the Jocist, Cardijn inspired, lay movements both historically and in the present day as well as the examining the rich tradition of Catholic Social teaching on the Church in the world of today. Articles cover a range of areas: the spirituality, methodology and the history of these traditions and movements in the Church and in society.

Editor: Hilary Dominic Regan

Editorial Board

- **Dr Kevin Ahern**, Professor of Religious Studies, Manhattan College, USA
- **Dr Ana Maria Bidegain**, Professor of Latin American Religions at Florida International University, USA
- **Fr Michael Deeb OP**, former IYCS Chaplain South Africa
- **Fr Mark James OP**, former National YCS Chaplain in South Africa, Eswatini
- **David Moloney**, professional historian, Cardijn Community Australia Executive Member
- **Dr Stefan Gigacz**, Secretary Cardijn Community, Australia

Business Manager, Editor and Publisher:
Mr Hilary Dominic Regan, ATF Press Publishing Group, PO Box 234, Brompton, SA 5007, Australia.
Email: hdregan@atf.org.au

ISBN	978-1-923006-08-9	soft
	978-1-923006-09-6	hard
	978-1-923006-10-2	epub
	978-1-923006-11-9	pdf

Published and edited by

Making a lasting impact

An imprint of the ATF Press Publishing Group
owned by ATF (Australia) Ltd.
PO Box 234
Brompton, SA 5007
Australia
ABN 90 116 359 963
www.atfpress.com
Making a lasting impact

Cardijn Studies: On the Church in the World of Today: Volume 4/2 2023

Table of Contents

Editorial   vii
     Hilary D Regan

1. Mark James OP Interview With Albert Nolan OP, 1985   1

2. Julie Frederikse Interview With Albert Nolan OP, 1985   15

3. Kairos Theology   39

4. The Eschatology of the Kairos Document   49

5. Integral Education   59

6. A Spirituality of Action   67

7. Biography of Albert Nolan OP   73

Cardijn Studies: On the Church in the World of Today: Volume 4/2 2023

Editorial

The photo on the front cover of this volume is of Albert Nolan OP and comes from around 1983 shortly after he served as National Chaplain in South Africa for the National Catholic Federation of Students (NCFS), a tertiary based student member movement of the International Movement of Catholic Students (IMCS). He was National Chaplain from 1973–1980. From 1977–1984, Nolan served as National Chaplain of the South African YCS (a member movement of the International YCS), which affiliated itself to the United Democratic Front (UDF) in South Africa.[1] The colours of the cover are those that were used by UDF, black, red and yellow.

The title of this volume, *Putting Right What Is Wrong*, comes from Nolan himself when he talks of the 'actions' of the YCS and of biblical justice in a 1980s interview, which is published in this collection.

Albert Nolan OP (1934–2022), a South African Dominican, joined the Order in the 1950s and was, in the 1970s and early 1980s, involved with various Cardijn inspired lay movements in South Africa, particularly student and post-graduate student movements in that country. He was a chaplain to various Catholic student bodies

---

1. 'The UDF was a South African popular front that existed from 1983 to 1991. The UDF comprised more than 400 public organizations including trade unions, students' unions, women's and parachurch organizations. The UDF's goal was to establish a "non-racial, united South Africa in which segregation is abolished and in which society is freed from institutional and systematic racism". Its slogan was "UDF Unites, Apartheid Divides". The Front was established in 1983 to oppose the introduction of the Tricameral Parliament by the white-dominated National Party government, and dissolved in 1991 during the early stages of the transition to democracy.' Taken from Wikipedia. Last accessed on 15 April 2023.

and a writer. He is best known for his *Jesus before Christianity*[2] book which was first published in English in 1976 (was translated into over a dozen other languages) and is still in print. He was involved in the writing of the 1985 *Kairos Document*[3] and worked with the Institute of Contextual Theology (ICT) in South Africa.

In the mid 1970s he went to Latin America for an international student conference and met Gustavo Gutiérrez (who later also became a Dominican), who was also involved with international student movements in the Catholic Church at that time.[4] The trip, and the writings of liberation theology he encountered around that time, were both an important influence as he explains in the 1985 interview with the South African Historical Archives (SAHA), which is published in this volume: 'A very important thing too, was a Theology of Liberation in Latin America. But even that, I started reading that gradually and then spent six weeks in Latin America in 1975 and that was very important to me.'

A number of other Dominicans in South Africa were also involved in the Jocist movements of formation as were Dominicans in France like Chenu, Congar and others in the twentieth century as well as other countries over the years. Thus Nolan was not alone in South Africa, nor internationally within the Dominicans, to be involved in lay movements of formation.

The link between Nolan's work and writings with the Jocist, Cardijn inspired, action based movements of formation, has not often been written up, alluded to, explained or detailed to any great extent in academic journals or publications, nor referred to by many theologians when examining contemporary theological trends. In the same way, the links between Gustavo Gutierrez's theology, and his involvement with the student movements, has seldomly been detailed or written about by those who have studied his work or liberation theology.

---

2. *Jesus before Christianity* (Maryknoll, NY: Orbis Books, 1976).
3. *Kairos Document* (Braamfontein: Skotaville, 1986).
4. The latest entry of the life and work of Gustavo Gutiérrez in Wikipedia makes the connection with the lay movements: 'He studied medicine and literature at the National University of San Marcos, where he also became involved with Catholic Action, which greatly influenced his theological arguments.' Last accessed on 10 March 2023

In this volume Nolan speaks in two interviews from the 1980s (one with fellow Dominican Mark James OP and another which is was recorded by Julie Frederikse and is in the files of the South African Historical Association) about his time with the student movements in South Africa, his theological development because of his involvement with the student movements, his visit to Latin America in the 1970s, the connections between liberation theology in Latin America and theology in South Africa in the Apartheid regime and of contextual theology. 'We talk about an option for the poor,[5] which might describe what I'm trying to do and describe what Latin American theologians and others are trying to do.' While noting differences between theologies of liberation in South Africa and Latin America, Nolan also links the work of the student movements, movements for justice in Latin America and South Africa and social analysis: 'But a social analysis of the structure of our society reveals a power relationship of oppressor and oppressed just as it does in Latin America, and many other countries.'

In the two interviews he speaks of leadership which developed based on 'action', often small actions in the student movements, where students take action to change and 'put right that which is wrong'.[6] There is the link between those small actions and actions at a larger scale in a time of 'struggle' against repression, oppression and witnessing suffering, poverty and inequality.

There are also two articles on the *Kairos Document* and *Kairos* theology. While not mentioning the links with 'action' based movements, in these articles Nolan refers to movements of change which are theologically grounded in responding to the 'signs of the times' and change in a society where one 'puts right something that is wrong'.

Finally, there are two pieces from 2003, some of his most recent pieces of writing and significant pieces as these were presentations that he gave to members of the student movements. In 2003, Nolan participated in an international meeting of IMCS, at a joint training session with the International YCS which was held in Barcelona,

---

5. The 'option for the poor', was a term used by the YCS and other international student movements beginning from the late 1970s and 1980s coming first from Latin America and then from various international meetings.
6. 'All the actions of YCS and CAM etc are always actions to try and put right something that's wrong.'

Spain. The first is on 'Integral Education', and the second 'A Spirituality of Action'.[7]

While Nolan, like Gutiérrez, never refers directly to the writings of Cardijn, it is clearly there as an influence throughout their writings, if one reads their work through the optic of the works of Joseph Cardijn, founder of the YCW. Nolan's interview with the SAHA speaks of a 'call to action', taking up the theme of Cardijn's small 148 page book, *A Challenge to Action*, first translated and published in English in 1955, and the other seminal small 178 page book by Cardijn entitled *Laymen into Action*.[8]

When asked in the SAHA interview about his achievements, Nolan uses language which is similar to Cardijn's when he speaks of the link between action and leadership,

> [T]he most important achievement of it is the building of leadership, and a good number of black and white leaders in the struggle have come out of YCS. The experience that they went through and all that has made them leaders and they're all over the place.

---

7. Nolan had been a participant in 1975 at the 28th Interfederal Assembly of the International Movement of Catholic Students held in Lima, Peru. There he met among the eighty student leaders who were present Gustavo Gutiérrez, the chaplain of the hosting movement in Peru, the *Unión Nacional de Estudiantes Católicos*, and Tissa Balasuriya, OMI, IMCS Asia regional chaplain. Albert Nolan, OP, was there as chaplain of the National Catholic Federation of Students (NCFS) in South Africa, a member Movement of the IMCS. He later attended a World Council of the IYCS in Valladolid, Spain, in 1978.

8. *Challenge to Action: Addresses of Joseph Cardijn,* edited by Eugene Langdale (Melbourne: Geoffrey Chapman, 1955); *Laymen into Action* (Melbourne: YCW Melbourne, 1964/Adelaide: ATF Press, 2017, and renamed *Laypeople into Action*). Using words reminiscent to the writings of Cardijn, and of much that has come out of the Jocist tradition Nolan said in one of the interviews in this volume: 'part of what NCFS, YCS and YCW did was precisely to bring faith and life together because they were separated'. In the other interview with fellow Dominican Mark James published in this volume he speaks of the difference between different bodies in the Catholic Church which he, Nolan, had been associated with. There were those whose interest more in spirituality and others, those in Cardijn inspired movements, where the interest was of a more theological in nature.

He goes on,

> . . .. now those are the things that build leadership. It is the fact that hundreds of times, you have done that, you've taken the initiative, you've involved other people in doing it, you found a way of doing it, when it didn't work you reviewed why it didn't work and again that's the stuff of which leaders are made. That's education.

Education and formation in the Jocist tradition are linked, and refer to the life of 'action', a life of 'putting right what is wrong'.

The late 1960s through to 1970s were years of radicalisation of the Jocist movements in many countries. The cause/s and form/s of the radicalisation differed from one country to another. In Asia, Latin America and South Africa there were similarities in how oppressive regimes reacted to those who challenged them. While Nolan saw similarities between South Africa and Latin America in particular, he also saw differences. Nolan points outs the use of theology by the Dutch Reformed Church in South Africa was one major difference between the two contexts, which was a significant difference to regimes in Latin America.[9] In some parts of the world, in Asia, Latin America, and South Africa student leaders in the YCS and leaders in the YCW were imprisoned, tortured, beaten and death threats came from the security forces or military at the behest of those in political power.[10]

By contrast, in Australia, for example (where the editor of *Cardijn Studies* journal lives), in that period, the YCS moved from being a rather classroom Catholic school based student movement to a more 'action' based radical movement, based on later what was articulated

---

9. 'There are some similarities in Latin America, but they haven't used Christianity and theology as obviously and intentionally as the South African regime has done, throughout the ages, with the Dutch Reformed Church say behind it in that kind of thing.'

10. In an article on Kairos theology in this volume, Nolan refers to large scale events that occurred against activists, in a wide spread manner, at the time of 1985 State of Emergency that was declared in South Africa in the following way: 'The crisis m 1985 was brought about by, on the one side, tyrannical repression (detentions, trials, killings, torture, bannings, propaganda, states of emergency) and, on the other side, all-out resistance (boycotts, strikes. uprisings, burnings and armed struggles). This was the *kairos* at that time.'

as and called the 'option for the poor' coming from statements at international meetings. Prior to that articulation it was centred on responses to events in Asia, and Vietnam in particular.

This radicalisation left many in the Australian Church hierarchy bewildered and uncomfortable, not understanding what was happening and questioning what had happened to a lay movement they had supported in many and different ways. This period was also of course linked to massive societal change as well as change within the Catholic Church at the time of Vatican II. Thus there was a confluence of different factors inside and outside of the Church.

For many in leadership positions in the YCS in Australia, while they knew of oppressive regimes in various parts of the world, including South Africa and Latin America, and were aware that for many in the world there was poverty and suffering, it was the relative geographical closeness of Asia and the Vietnam War, and the fact that many young Australians were conscripted and fought in that war, which was the focus of the movements and was a significant part of the process of radicalisation of many in leadership roles in the YCS and the YCW.

This collection then, is a prelude to what will be a larger volume of talks and articles by Nolan to be published at a later date (provisionally 2024), and covering a range of topics, along with a volume of essays in honour of his life and work (including articles about his work with the student movements) entitled *Reluctant Pophet: Tributes to Albert Nolan OP* (ATF Press, 2023). These two other volumes will add to this publication detailing the work of Albert Nolan.

At the same time, this publication will be the beginning, we hope, of bringing to the fore the link between the work for justice in South Africa and liberation theology with the lay movements in the Catholic Church. Read the present volume from the optic of the writings of Cardijn and one will make continuous and deep connections between the writings of Nolan and also Gutiérrez. Likewise with this optic, it is possible for many and profound connections to be made between liberation theology in South Africa and Latin America, particularly in the works of Nolan and Gutiérrez, with the See-Judge-Act method of the Jocist lay movements and their YCS background in particular. This is a field of research that is yet to be studied in depth by scholars, and yet as will be seen in the pages that follow, the connections are there for those who come from a Jocist background.

ATF Press acknowledges and is very grateful for the work undertaken by Dominicans in South Africa, some of whom were members of the student movements, for collecting these pieces, bringing them to our attention. In like manner, we acknowledge Kevin Ahern, who from 2003–2007 served as president of IMCS, for bringing these two papers that Nolan gave at a meeting in Barcelona to our attention.

ATF Press would like to thank Mark James OP for allowing the publication of his interview with Albert Nolan and to the other publishers, and the IMCS in Paris, for allowing us to reproduce Nolan's previously published pieces and, in the case of the last two IMCS papers, unpublished papers. In all instances only light editing has occurred with the texts which follow so as to allow Nolan to speak in his own words as and when these pieces were recorded or written.

Hilary D Regan
June 2023

Cardijn Studies: On the Church in the World of Today: Volume 4/2 2023

1
Mark James OP Interview With Fr Albert Nolan in Mondeor, Johannesburg on 4 May 2005

Mark James was introduced to the Cardijn movements when he was a university student at Wits University from 1981–1985. He was involved in the National Catholic Federation of Students (NCFS) and became conference organiser in 1985. He also joined Young Christian Students (YCS) while at university. He later became National Chaplain of YCS from 1999–2004 and also reacquainted himself with the IMCS affiliated Association of Catholic Tertiary Students (ACTS) as chaplain at the University of KwaZulu-Natal (UKZN) from 2014–2016. The interview was done with Albert Nolan as part of my research for his Masters thesis on the lay Dominicans who declined in influence after the Second Vatican Council in contrast to the Cardijn-inspired student and worker movements.

Mark: I just wanted to ask you in terms of your own involvement with the lay Dominicans. What were you involved in? What was happening at the time? What attracted you to the lay Dominicans? And to what extent did that include your decision to become a Dominican yourself?

Albert: OK, first I was a lay Dominican from I think about 1951–53 because in '54 I became a novice in Stellenbosch. So I think it was '51 to '53 and that's only about three years to begin with. Before I can explain something about why I became a lay Dominican I need to go a little bit further back, say for a year or two before that - it was a year. I had already become much more involved in the Church. I was in the Legion of Mary and that was very formative in the sense that you met and you had prayers together but you had a very well organised apostolate. So you would visit hospitals and sell *Southern Crosses* on the street, you would visit lapsed Catholics and things like that. That

1

was the kind of apostolate ministry [where] work for your neighbour came in. I also worked for the youth club, and was on the committee of the youth club and then at one stage maybe after I became a tertiary, we called it tertiary in those days, I was also beginning to be trained in the Catholic Evidence Guild (CEG). The CEG came from England, and it was the kind of thing that Vincent Mc Nabb preached at Hyde Park corner and it was . . . a lay organisation that would preach on street corners, not only in Hyde Park but in other places—in Cape Town we did it outside the OK Bazaars actually. On a Sunday night somebody would preach and people would gather and they would ask questions and he would answer the questions and things like that. Then we were trained to do that, you went to them, you listened to what somebody did and they trained you on how to do it. I didn't get very far with it but I say all that because that was the ministry, that was the apostolate, the kind of thing to do. What was lacking, if you want to call it lacking, was some kind of spirituality. I'm not quite sure anyone would have used the word spirituality as such but . . . OK let's say you felt the need for some kind of spirituality. The place for that would be, for example, would be the tertiaries, and so as Billy D'Arcy and Guy Ruffel went . . . No, Billy D' Arcy was already a tertiary. So Guy Ruffel and I were invited by Billy D'Arcy to join the chapter in St Mary's convent that is, behind the cathedral. We met every, it can't be every Saturday, but it was on Saturdays anyway perhaps once a month but I think it was more frequent than that, and what we would do in the afternoons was the main thing that happened was that we would say the Lady Office and then there would be a Dominican priest there and he would give a talk. Then we might discuss some things or get some information about Dominicans and things like that. Now it was quite formally organised in the sense that you had a rule and became a novice and you had a novice master. Billy D'Arcy was my novice master and you were a novice for a year. Apart from the chapter meetings, as it was called, you had to meet with the novice master regularly and he told you more about being a Dominican, and prayer and things like that, explain more about the Office perhaps and told you more about what the promises were about and went through the rule with you. That was a big thing to go through. Now the lay Dominicans or the tertiaries as such never did any apostolates or ministries. That wasn't strange because you went to your parish to do that. You went to the Legion of Mary or a youth club or something like that.

That's where your ministries and your apostolates came in. But the lay Dominicans never organised ministries or apostolates in that chapter. By the way that chapter, there was a famous Major Mehan you might come across, Madge Green and various people like that. I don't remember too many of them now. Anyway, so why did we go there, what was it? Because [it was] the only kind of concept one had of how you nourished your spirituality, how you worked towards Christian perfection. Because the image of Christian perfection and contemplation was of course through the monastery, the monk, the prior, the priory and things like that. But perhaps I ought to say that part of our practice was that we would go to the priory, that was very important actually, we would go to the priory for weekends we would go to the priory for retreats, for one or two day retreats. That was extremely important. There was a centre somewhere we went to, and then one of those priests, Hildebrand James, was the chaplain I think, was called a tertiary chaplain. I was saying about spirituality, that what was understood to be the way you had a spirituality. It's pretty medieval in a certain sense because to reach Christian perfection you had to follow a Rule and that Rule, the principal thing in that Rule was: commitment to the Lady Office. If you were in the monastery, or the First Order of the Dominicans or the Sisters, you would say the full Divine Office. So that's how it was understood. At that particular time too a big interest was just developing and growing, it was exactly those years, in Thomas Merton. Thomas Merton was an icon of holiness and perfection and the rest of it, going into monastery, silences, contemplation, prayer and all that kind of thing. Nobody understood a totally different form of spirituality except perhaps the Legion of Mary's prayers and that was a whole long 'one prayer after the other' and the rosary. So at the Legion of Mary meeting you would say the rosary first at the beginning of the meeting followed by a whole lot of prayers and a handbook, which was in some senses like a Rule, and those prayers we had to say at the meetings and the statutes had to be there and how they all came to be, all those details and [what] you took on, how you found out what it was we had to do, which were always from the priest. We had to ask the priest what was needed and if people got tasks we did them two by two and came back and reported and that was also a tightly organised thing. You always had to report that you had done it and what happened. So there was a bit of a spirituality there by using the rosary and some of the prayers.

Mark: Sounds like the spirituality was linked very much into doing the prayers and the things like that but not really focused on things that were action-based. What was the relationship between the tertiary schools and the Catholic Action or organisations that were more involved with working for the good of your neighbour like YCW and YCS groups? Were there some tertiaries involved with social programmes?

Albert: Well, the only one that I can remember was YCW. Bernard Meager, for example, was a Dominican tertiary. His action wasn't in the Legion Mary, it was to join YCW. He died of a brain tumour at twenty-one and he was a good person, a holy person, but he worked in YCW. But nobody saw that as terribly different as working in the Legion of Mary or something like that because even the YCW in those days weren't fighting Apartheid. Now that perhaps, you asked about 'Why didn't you see this as working for the good of your neighbour?' but we did see it as working for the good of your neighbour but it was for the individual neighbour. So if you ask: 'Well, why not the social dimension?' I think the first thing about it is that people didn't have a social consciousness, so you didn't think in terms of 'what about the social dimensions? What about the social injustice?' I can't even remember that word being used 'social justice' or things like that. It just didn't come in so that your religion and your spirituality, everything, was so totally individualistic that you didn't even recognise the social dimension and, of course, a lot of people who weren't Christians also didn't recognise the social dimension. The other thing was that even in YCW, I don't think that at that stage the social dimensions were that clear, it was still working to help workers and the individuals really.

Mark: Were you aware of the changes happening in society in terms of the Apartheid laws and their implications? [Though] The Cape was a little [more] isolated than Johannesburg, you were still liberal in approach than other parts of the country?

Albert: But we had some, maybe not as much as the rest of the country, but that wasn't the issue. The issue was 'that was politics' and politics was not [for the church]. You had to . . . you had a choice. If you wanted to be part of that you had to be a kind of a politician in some form or another, not a parliament politician but a politician involved in protesting or something like that.

Mark: Was this considered as part of spirituality?

Albert: No, no, not at all, not at all. In fact...

Mark: Or Christian perfection?

Albert: No. Not at all.

Mark: Unless it was sort of very pro-Catholic movement.

Albert: But even that had to start around the 1950s. The first time that Catholics in any way spoke up about it was Bishop Henneman in about 1956 or 1957. I remember that in the youth club we were planning talks, we used to get together and we wanted to plan a talk, someone would come in and talk about Apartheid and the priest said 'No, that's politics. You can't talk about politics in any way' and I remember that we were fed up about that but that's as far as it went. So there was no way in which the tertiaries were going to say anything different. It may be difficult to believe but it was just regarded as a another world... So the growth of social consciousness for some people was almost always involved or almost always arose through some kind of experience of the suffering of black people because of the system, because of Apartheid. So, for myself it would be when we started going into townships, even coloured townships and seeing what was happening there and what the people were staying in, but that was all after the 1950s.

Mark: And were there coloured members on the board of the tertiaries or only white?

Albert: No, no they were all whites.

Mark: Even though there was a chapter in Stellenbosch?

Albert: I don't remember, there could've been. Then you have to say which time you are talking about in about these 1950s there was none. You see I'm quite sure that later towards the 60s there must have been coloureds running a parish but this time, no. Not that people were necessarily objective. It's a very strange thing to try and explain. I think coloured members would have been welcomed but nobody thought about it, nobody thought that they become tertiaries as well, no black people wanted to become, I don't think, because it was a white group. It's difficult to understand how some of these things were never even averted; we just didn't think about them or question it. But there's another dimension to it and this is justice was not associated with church, Christianity, with faith, with Christian perfection. Justice was another thing; justice was something for employers or people like that. I can remember later on once saying something about justice to somebody in the audience saying that 'How can you as a priest talk about justice - it's a communist word?' It's as bad as justice in a communist. So although at this time there were already social encyclicals people did not know what they were. YCW started with *Rerum Novarum*. So ignorance was a big thing.

Mark: Do you think that the spirituality of the tertiaries was encouraged when joining the chapter for example, because often they used to [receive a talk from the] priests. From what I've read and what I try to understand is that it was very much focused on learning from the priest. There was no, like personal growth or development or a sense of one's own appropriation of the faith or anything like that. An admiration society of the priests, would that be a factor?

Albert: No, I didn't think that you would say it was an admiration society because we would criticise the priests. It was just that they were the experts who were not thought to be any different from a doctor, they were supposed to be the experts. You could learn some of those things but just in the same way as you couldn't compete with a doctor on medical matters, so in the same way you couldn't compete with a priest in spiritual matters. No, although we didn't like what some people had said or that some people didn't have answers to questions etc. That is why we liked the Dominican Order because they did discuss and they did have answers to questions. Perhaps a concrete example of this, I remember going to the parish priests with a question about hell. 'How can there be such a loving God but there's a place like hell?' and he said 'You don't ask questions like that'. Then I went to the Dominicans to ask the same question and they said, 'No, no, that's good, let's sit down and let's talk about that etc'. So that in my mind was a very big difference between the Dominicans and the secular priests, you could ask questions, you could discuss. So it wasn't an admiration of priests as such. No, this is not true. They were just people who knew about these things and you could go and talk to them and discuss things with them, bring questions to them. Spirituality was prayer, was discipline, saying prayers and saying prayers. There was mental prayer, oh yes there was that, but not in the sense as today with a mantra or anything of that sort. I remember Thomas Merton was already having an influence. So silence and solitude and those things . . . We used to go to Stellenbosch as a priory for silence, for solitude, for private prayer and things like that. So that was already something that was the contemplation that was part of one's holiness and Christian perfection.

Mark: Now let's move from your experiences as a tertiary to when you were a Dominican in Stellenbosch. What memories do you have of the tertiaries and what contributions did they make to the life of the priory? What was the life of a tertiary in Cape Town as far as you remember? Did they make any important contributions to the life of the church?

Albert: No, I don't think so. What I just said carried on when I was already in Stellenbosch at the priory. There would've been people who came to visit, came on the weekends and came for retreats and things like that.

Mark: Who was a visitor?

Albert: Oh, OK. It would have been Dougie Wiseman . . . it was often a stepping-stone to join the Order.

Mark: What was the understanding of that is it true that many of the tertiaries have, if you could call it an inferiority complex, that they weren't proper Dominicans? That somehow the real life was actually to be a priest.

Albert: Yes, there was that. Remember you were called the Third Order and to be called to join the First Order was the same thing but much more intensely and deeply and fully. I remember that at first what I wanted to be was a diocesan priest, or simply a priest, and the way I would have conceived it was because I enjoyed doing the work of the Legion of Mary and the youth club and that sort of thing. But I worked in a bank and I wanted to do ministry and apostolic work full-time. That's how we saw it, doing church work full-time and that's what it meant to be a priest. The women amongst us, the girls who wanted to do it full-time, went to the convent to do church work. I wouldn't, by the way, see it as church work only, as simply as that. I mean there was the altar boy and things like that might have been more church work. Actually going to hospitals—even though we were told by the priest, where to go and where we were needed—selling *Southern Crosses* and all that kind of thing was not really church work. It was serving your neighbour, it was doing good to your neighbour rather than doing just church work. I mean to go visit people in hospitals wasn't like being an altar server being in a tertiary.

Mark: It wasn't liturgical. So there was a sense of ministry, a sense of apostolate.

Albert: Yes, yes.

Mark: Later when you became a provincial, it was in the 1970s in 1976, and they, lay Dominicans, were really battling at that point where they lost some sort of vision about who they were and Vatican II became a major challenge for them. One would have thought it would have encouraged the lay Dominicans because of the emphasis on lay apostolates, but in fact it seemed to undermine them. Do you have any memories with regard to that? What happened at that point that seemed to put the lay Dominicans in crisis?

Albert: Well, the first was that no young people were joining in, they were elderly and there was a generation gap and the younger people who came into this kind of practice were bored by it and didn't find it . . . Ja well, they found the old people boring and what the old people talked about was not interesting and all the rest was boring. So there was a generation gap.

Mark: What was boring, the activities of the lay Dominicans? Because they look actively involved in the activities of the parish ministries?

Albert: That's right. It wasn't so much that as the old people weren't interesting, the younger people would obviously be interested in trying to change things in some way or another and they would talk about 'couldn't we revise the rule' and things like that. Then the old people want nothing to do with that. So there was a generation gap but it wasn't just, that was one element of it. There was a huge chapter, it was very difficult. I remember that in Cape Town and here we thought the only thing is to start a new movement for young people. I remember that very clearly and we tried to do that there and we tried to do that here but it didn't work. We couldn't get the young and we couldn't find a priest to chaplain that either. So what happened is you worked with young people who were not interested in being Christians, so you worked with YCS, YCW, NCFS, CASA, CHIRO, youth clubs or something. But none of those were interested, so you had a new generation that might be interested in See-Judge-Act and things like that. They were not interested in a kind of monastic spirituality thing of the lay Dominicans and associated that with old people and pre-Vatican II.

Mark: Do you think, what would you say was the shift in spirituality? Many of the young lay people in fact had deep desire for spirituality which maybe, in fact, wasn't that different from the people in the 1950s. What was the difference in nature of the spiritualities?

Albert: I think the first thing to say is that they actually gave up on the word 'spirituality'. When I was.... The YCS and YCW, nobody ever talked about 'spirituality', what they talked about was theology and I think that's an interesting kind of shift. In the lay Dominicans that I first joined you never talked about theology that was a subject you studied in the seminary. But we all talked about spirituality in the form you can call Christian perfection. But later on this wasn't [acceptable], spirituality was regarded as a very individualistic thing, as me and God, and spirituality was the born-again people and they just had to pray about it and problems would go away etc. Theology was saying how justice was done and that God was on the side of the poor and things like that. So theology was much more [used] . . . and Jesus, very much so but not spirituality as such. But there was a sort of spirituality as you say, it's just that there wasn't a name there. The spirituality was, I think, the experience people would talk about would be the experience of singing and dancing at mass, that kind of thing. The excitement of it, the excitement of a conference and planning together, doing things together, that would have been very much spirituality. So if you asked the NCFS people in those days where they found God, if you like, it would be at an exciting Mass.

Mark: There was also a period where there was a great[er] political awareness than previously.

Albert: Oh ja. By this time there was, because you jumped to when I was the provincial. Political awareness had grown in time and that's a whole long story on its own too. The political awareness grew too among students, black and white, and there were priests who encouraged that very much in the true fashion of Colin Collins to Didicus

Diego, a Franciscan, and people like that. Then I came doing that as well. So yes there was a social consciousness between the lot and at first, aside from Didicus who was an exception, and he had no successor. When I first came to the chaplaincy there was no theology. It was all politics. It was all social analysis or maybe social realities, so that every conference had speakers, none of them were priests. And the speakers would come and talk about the situation, about the politics. I introduced theology so that later on priests would even talk about Jesus and theology and you know even some of the older students would do that too but it had been lost.

Mark: Do you know the reason why . . . because there were some priests who were still chaplains to the tertiaries or the lay Dominicans but they never really brought See-Judge-Act or their political consciousness into the lay Dominicans? Do you know the reason why that never took off? Was it the nature of the people involved?

Albert: Yes, I think so. The tertiaries wouldn't have been interested in that.

Mark: Was there also not also possibly a compartmentalisation of action and prayer? There were people who lived the spirituality in one area went to church and then dealt with... there was no like interrelationship faith and life.

Albert: That's right but part of what NCFS, YCS and YCW did was precisely to bring faith and life together because they were separated.

Mark: So in the tertiaries this would never have been brought in, it would never have been reflected on?

Albert: I didn't know Advocate Vieyra, he was an exception. I remember him but I can't seem to remember any other tertiaries . . . Madge Green would have had some sense of it and would have been active.

Mark: There were also people like Jimmy and Joan Stewart who were tertiaries but never really fitted in to the tertiary mould where their interest was primarily social transformation. They never really were part of the chapter.

Albert: I think they're a good example of how it was often because they knew Dominican priests and admired some Dominican priests. It was because of that that they would have been tertiaries but not in justice as such, though Dominicans are open to that kind of thing.

There was a scene change in different ways and Vatican II was one very good example of that change. Spirituality, theology and the introduction of justice was one. So there were big changes.

Mark: What's interesting about that is that it seems to be detrimental effect on the lay Dominicans rather than the encouragement of them. They all seemed to die out and it seemed to throw them into crisis rather than growth.

Albert: Most of them weren't able to make the adjustment. In the same way convents emptied out and many priests left, for the same kind of reasons, people couldn't adapt so they would drop out.

Mark: To what extent had it to do with this idea of that it was a religious life that was integral to people's spirituality that somehow you became more spiritual by being religious, a Dominican?

Albert: By being, but it was also by living that kind of life by the discipline, by the Rule, by the prayers, by the vows, that's just how they made it holy.

Mark: You saying it wasn't necessary under Vatican II to have the rules and laws to encourage them to have a spiritual life?

Albert: I think Vatican II opened the windows to freedom and that there were other ways of doing things and other ways living and that kind of thing. That the religious life wasn't a superior way of life and you could still be a saint and married and things like that.

Mark: Going back to what we spoke about earlier, regarding social consciousness. What does it mean to have a social conscience or consciousness?

Albert: The social conscience, generally speaking, affects the people who are trying to be spiritual as well because they can be blind to it. But you are not blinded simply by your spirituality as such. You are blinded by the lack of social consciousness and you don't see social problems. One way of putting it, when people suffered they didn't see that there was a possibility of changing the structures of society. There was no concept of structural change. So for example if you take slavery. Obviously slavery was not Christian, it was against the faith, but for Paul there was no possibility of changing slavery as a structure of society. It was unthinkable it was unimaginable. So, he didn't do it or say this has got to change because it didn't enter anyone's head. It was only later with Wilberforce that it was seen that it is possible to change that structure so there isn't slavery. So there are lots of examples of that, the whole struggle for social justices develops out of things like the revolutions, the French Revolution, the American Revolution, the Russian Revolution. Whatever you may say about them, they showed that the structures of power can be changed and before you could only change the person on top of the structure, the king, and the dictator but you couldn't change the whole system. It was unthinkable, and even for Thomas Aquinas is was unthinkable. Justice meant the prince had to be just, but to have no prince was unthinkable, unimaginable and impossible to do. If you imagined it there was no means or power to do that.

Mark: So, in some senses when we talk in a Christian light in terms of contemplation because contemplation, the way I understand it, is to come to a new awareness or a new awareness of your consciousness and to come consciousness beyond the limitations of our society at the present moment. In a sense spirituality doesn't always allow you to do that, come to that new consciousness, spirituality in a sense even limits us in consciousness.

Albert: No. Spirituality should help us open and should make us want to get beyond selfishness, etc. but we may not see the way beyond that socially, and there may not be a way beyond that socially.

Mark: At that period? Like ecological for example, recently there was an ecological consciousness, the whole new paradigm of the universe for example.

Albert: Yes, that's right and until you had trade unions and things like that workers were in a hopeless situation. To get to the point of the Dominicans not having a social consciousness, not having a social consciousness, we never imagined that Apartheid could change. Apartheid was the reality. In the thinking of some people, the individual thinking of some people, the idea that you could have a structural change came about.

Mark: What is different though is that there was a small church that did develop a social consciousness? Why is it that they developed social consciousness like YCS, NCFS and not groups like tertiaries for example? What is it about their make up or their spirituality or their organisation that didn't allow them to develop?

Interview With Mark James OP 13

Albert: The process by which those people who did stand up got to it was conscientisation and it was making people aware of things and making people aware of the suffering that was happening, making people aware of the fact that it can change. Now that didn't get through to most older people, black and white and it didn't get through to tertiaries certainly. It was more likely to get through to younger people in universities, who were suffering already perhaps. So the new thinking didn't reach tertiaries, but I think what most can immediately say is that in so far as it did start seeping through and that's my experience certainly. Then its link with the gospel became obvious to some people immediately, but then we had to have the social consciousness as well as the gospel to link it.

Mark: To what extent was there also a limitation in the use of scripture to help people understand it? Because from what I hear there was talks given by priests that was often not helping them. Then the consciousness of priests was limited to not seeing that their role was to try and help people come to their new consciousness or awareness of themselves through scripture, like a lot of these youth groups they practiced scripture.

Albert: That's right because when you went back to scripture and Jesus and gospels and all the rest you saw that justice was relevant. No, the kind of talks as you said the priests gave about was pietistic, devotional or speculative theology is the other word, questions about hell and other expert opinion of biblical movement of reading the Bible became important and things like that. I remember even at Mass we had the gospel, well, if you were a bit more conscientious we would call it scripture. Ja, so it was . . . to finish what I was going to say is that my mother was very good and kind and all that kind of thing to black people, to poor people and all that kind of thing and felt very sorry for them and their plight. Actually I remember the words very much, she would say 'One day there's going to be a civil war about how they are treated etc . . . but remember don't mix with them.' It was a total contradiction of course but not mixing, that was the society, that was the custom, that was the social thinking. It would've been a bit like being sympathetic towards prostitutes who were also in our streets. But you weren't allowed to mix with them.

Mark: Thank you very much.

Cardijn Studies: On the Church in the World of Today: Volume 4/2 2023

2
Julie Frederikse Interview With Albert Nolan OP in 1985[1]

Julie Frederikse: I would like to actually ask you some things about background and how—really briefly—how you got involved? Let me just start by back-talking and ask you to say what you just said.

If someone were to say to you, is this a valid topic, why would you say you think it is?

Albert Nolan: No, I think it is a valid topic, the white resistance in South Africa. I think it is important that it be known, first of all, especially because in my experience outside of South Africa it's seldom known.

The struggle is seen in simple black and white terms which I think is not entirely true. The resistance is often a class thing to start off with, and a question of who one sides with, in terms of siding with the oppressors or the oppressor and whites have that choice—whether they're going to side with the oppressor or the oppressed.

I think it is sufficient that there are a good number of whites who have not sided with the oppressor but sided with the oppressed. And I think that's an important fact in the struggle in South Africa.

In other words, although race is the most prominent part of the struggle, the whole issue in the final analysis is not simply about race.

It's about oppression. And when it's about oppression, well, you can side with or against oppression, whatever your colour may be.

---

1. Interview from The Julie Frederikse Collection (AL2460_A14.17.1), South African History Archive (SAHA); published in *The Unbreakable Thread: Non-racialism in South Africa* by Julie Frederikse (Ravan Press, South Africa; Zed Books, UK; Indiana University Press, US; Anvil Press, Zimbabwe (1990); SAHA (2015).

Julie Frederikse: And do you think there are whites inside South Africa who don't know about white resistance in South Africa or who don't realise? Or do you think that they know something more about it?

Albert Nolan: Yes, I think there probably are whites who don't know that. On the whole they do, but they don't know much about it, but they think of it as there are a few white communists around the place.

And they know for example that there are white people in the ANC. They've often heard of people like Joe Slovo or somebody like that.

So, in the minds of most white people, there is the fact that there's some of these white communists who go around agitating.

But on the whole, I obviously think that it's very, very important that they should know about it, know more about it and have more accurate knowledge of white resistance. Yes.

Julie Frederikse: OK. Let me take you back. I'm interested to know a bit about your background, and how you grew to have your political views and personal ideological views that you did? Where do you come from?

Albert Nolan: Well, I'm born in Cape Town. I am fourth generation white South African I should think. I come from a white working class background and worked in a bank for four years. My father was a carpenter, so I went up the scale, so to speak. To be bank clerk for four years.

And then I became a priest. Now, my conscientisation has to do with being a Dominican priest. There are several factors to that.

Perhaps one of them is an understanding of my faith in religion as starting from the fact of suffering, suffering in the world, the nature of the suffering, why people suffer—the fact of starvation and why people are starving, getting one to issues like oppression etc.

Now, that has always been very important for me and I should think that is an important starting point for me.

It's an important starting point for me in my own theological studies of what religion is about, what the Bible is about and so forth.

And on the other hand if you have a concern and interest for suffering people, you're likely to mix with them, you're likely to listen to them, you're likely to side with them eventually.

It is of course a gradual process. It's difficult to describe all the stages or anything like that. With that sort of principle, if you like, behind it of concern with people who are suffering and concern to do something about it and religion is about that kind of thing. One gradually becomes more conscientised and you learn more of what is happening as you discover more of why it's happening, and you discover more of what the Bible really means.

Julie Frederikse: Except for most people don't really go through that gradually—was there anything specific, was there any turning point that you could pull out to say that this is an example of something that opened your eyes?

Albert Nolan: There was no big dramatic change that I know of. I can mention some things that were very important.

One is working with students. I was a student chaplain for a long time. I therefore faced the questions that students asked. The questions that students asked about politics and the questions that students asked about the Bible.

So, I was faced with those questions and having to try and find answers to those questions. So, working with students, first of all white university students, then black and white university students and eventually black school kids as well. That certainly had an conscientising effect.

But again it's not one dramatic moment change, but it's working over a good number of years with such people working with such people that had an influence, ja.

Julie Frederikse: Do you have a recollection of when you first heard about black figures in politics? When you first heard mention of Mandela and the ANC? Do you have any memory of how that first was made clear to you?

Albert Nolan: No, I can't remember when I first heard exactly of the ANC or Mandela. One grows up with that. Whet would have been more important—I would have heard about it first of all in a very pejorative sense and a very bad way, and then gradually come to realise that it wasn't so bad or to change one's mind about it.

But again, I'm afraid I haven't got any nice dramatic stories of change or conversion, it's mostly gradual.

A very important thing too, was a Theology of Liberation in Latin America. But even that, I started reading that gradually and then spent six weeks in Latin America in 1975 and that was very important to me.

But, even before that I had been reading Theology of Liberation texts before that.

Julie Frederikse: Where did you go in 1975?

Albert Nolan: Basically I went to a conference, a Catholic student conference in Lima, in Peru. But on the way, I passed through Brazil and on my way back from Lima I passed through Santiago and Chile and Buenos Aires.

Then I met some of the of the Theologians of Liberation and students and so forth.

Julie Frederikse: Had you before that thought about in the context of South Africa?

Albert Nolan: Oh yes, very much.

Julie Frederikse: An when you say this gradual movement, was that going through a stage of liberalism? You grew from being unaware to being a liberal to . . .

Albert Nolan: Yes, definitely, I definitely went through a stage of liberalism.

Julie Frederikse: But most people would not move there and if they moved there they'd stay there.

Albert Nolan: Ja. The movement from being a liberal to being, what shall we call it, being more radical, is something that has interested me for a long time—how people take that step and why they take that step.

I felt I did myself. It's very difficult to account for exactly, but a great deal of it is simply information, a great deal of it is for example—it's one thing to do something about it, another thing to know why there are poor people.

So, social analysis I would say is an extremely important factor in moving from one to the other. Open mindedness is obviously important there so you don't get stuck.

And then just generally experience of people. People you mix with and know, talk to and learn from, I would say that makes a difference too.

The big stumbling block for very many Christian liberals is theology. That they have a way of understanding what their Christian faith is that will prevent you from taking the step from liberal to radical.

And I think that one of the advantages I had was that theology was the subject, theology was one of the things I was thinking about, questioning and trying to understand better, and that meant perhaps that I was less likely to get stuck in a liberal phase.

Julie Frederikse: It's interesting that you say there can actually be a block—the theology.

Albert Nolan: Oh, decidedly so. Theology is my particular hobbyhorse, my interest, the thing that I do most about and I'm convinced that it is extremely important and that one of the reasons why the churches can't move any further, more deeply into the struggle, more effectively into the struggle at the moment is because in South Africa we don't have an adequate theology to do that.

We don't have an adequate way of accounting for why we should do that, why we must do it and one of the differences between South Africa [and] find say, Latin America, is that in Latin America, as people begin to get involved, there was current a new fashionable theology that made sense of what you were doing and that made sense of taking the next step.

But we don't have that, and that's one of our big lacks.

Julie Frederikse: And do you think if that's one of the lacks, do you see that changing?

Albert Nolan: Well, yes, there are numbers of people trying to [do] something about that and the whole institute for Contextual Theology that I'm working for tries to do that, to provide a South African theology, a contextual theology in that sense, to help people to see that their faith doesn't mean, or doesn't have to mean what they think it means—doesn't have the kind of constraints that it appears to have.

And that in fact it challenges one to do differ[ent] things from what one might have expected. And that that's all thoroughly biblically grounded.

Julie Frederikse: Can you tell me a bit more about your history in the Dominican Order? A couple of people have told me about various junctures, but can you tell me?

Albert Nolan: OK. I'm a Dominican and I became a Dominican at the beginning of 1954 and studied first in Stellenbosch where we had a seminary, and then two years in Rome.

I came back from there and I was a lecturer in our seminary in Stellenbosch. I gradually did various other jobs and ended up as a student chaplain and then was made what is known as the Provincial of Southern Africa, which means the person being responsible for the Dominicans in that area, the Southern African area.

That was an election. I was elected to that and I did two terms of office, two terms of four years, I did that for eight years.

When I was appointed provincial I came to Johannesburg—the headquarters of the Dominican Order is in Johannesburg. Before that I'd always been in the Cape.

[In] 1983 at an international meeting of Dominicans, I was elected to be the what is called the Master General, the title of the person who's responsible internationally for all Dominicans.

According to our rules and regulations, one can decline such an election but then you have to give your reasons for declining and then the assembly vote again about whether they accept your reasons or not, because you might give totally trivial reasons.

I gave my reasons as being the importance of the work in South Africa, particularly the theological work in the struggle in South Africa and the assembly accepted my reasons unanimously. And so I came back again.

Now normally that would not have been a particularly important event—but it was blown up in the newspapers, in Europe particularly, partly because it just hadn't happened before, partly because I am a South African and a white South African and I mentioned Apartheid in my reasons for not taking it up; all of which made it newsworthy.

Julie Frederikse: Tell me a bit more about it—I mean did you at all think of taking it up? I mean it would have been important.

Albert Nolan: No. I didn't hesitate at all. I believed subsequently someone's produced a play on the BBC about the election and my not taking it up, etc, etc. It caught the imagination of people in a strange sort of way.

And according to this play, I come back home and things go very badly and turn against me and all the rest and then I begin to think maybe I should have taken that and not stayed back here, and there's another twist which I'd forgotten at the moment where things go well again anyway, and then I'm back in South Africa.

Which is just so unlike me or my reasons that it's totally laughable. I didn't want to take it and I've never regretted for a moment that I didn't take it.

It was, I think even the romanticising of it and making it a big thing and people talking about it, is just a symptom of the very thing that I was fighting and that is to say that what happened was that there is a particular job that needs to be done which is to a certain extent an administrative job, which is a certain kind of leadership job.

But it has an enormous amount of prestige attached to it.

Now, one of the things I was rejecting, was the prestige attached to it, and saying 'we've got to lo look at this as a job. It's no different from any other job that I could do.' And I've got to compare it with the job that I'm doing in South Africa without any thought of prestige of either of them.

It's got nothing to do with promotion, it's got nothing to do with prestige. It's two jobs. And I must ask which am I most suited to, or which does God want me to do, to put it like that, or where would I be most effective?

And to me, it was absolutely obvious that I'd be more effective in the South African situation with my background and the things I've been able to do, and that someone else could do the other job.

So, to me it was no different from deciding whether I was going to teach theology in the university or work for the ICT or parish or something like that. It's deciding on a job.

Now, people have romanticised it because it's got all that prestige attached, because one is elected to it etc. Now that's, as I said, precisely what I was asking people not to do take into consideration and end asking our Chapter, as it's called, of the assembly to just look at it as two jobs and say now anybody in their right mind would see that I'm better suited to the job in South Africa than the other one. And that somebody else can do the other one, but not as easily find someone to do the job that I want to carry on doing in South Africa.

To me it's as simple as that. There was no problem about it. I had no regrets about it, there's no question of thinking of maybe I made a mistake and should have gone to do it, because that kind of issue about the prestige or something like that is precisely what I'm fighting against, precisely what I reject. The prestige of that job—no there's no question about the job.

Julie Frederikse: Do you mean what you are fighting about in South Africa?

Albert Nolan: Yes, because one of the most important things in terms of values and values of the Bible, or Christian values, etc is precisely that one doesn't go for status, prestige, for top things, for success, for achievement in that sense of going to the top.

Christianity is all about not doing that, but serving people in whatever ways it is and it doesn't matter whether I'm on top or where one is, [it's about] how can I serve people most effectively?

If I felt that l could serve people most effectively by being Master-General, then I would have done it, wouldn't have hesitated to do it. But I was not convinced of that.

The issue I'm trying to say here is there were two possible jobs you could do without regard to the relationship of the one to the other in terms of prestige and status.

And that, it seems to me, the man who wrote this play for example and many others, have not understood.

Julie Frederikse: Do you know who it was who wrote that play?

Albert Nolan: Desmond O'Grady, or O'Brady or something like that. I think is he a BBC correspondent or something like that? In Rome? I haven't met the man.

Julie Frederikse: Was it a televised play?

Albert Nolan: I am told so, yes. I believe so.

Julie Frederikse: You haven't heard?

Albert Nolan: No. I have only heard about it from other people who've seen it. Might have been a radio play, mind you, I'm not too sure, I have just heard about it.

Julie Frederikse: And you wouldn't know anyone who I could try and get it through?

Albert Nolan: No. The person who told me about it had heard it from someone else.

Julie Frederikse: And the name of the conference that elected you?

Albert Nolan: Every four years we have an international meeting of Dominicans which is called a General Chapter. And this was the General Chapter of 1983.

Julie Frederikse: And I would only use this to show the way you feel misrepresented. But do you have any of those clippings?

Albert Nolan: The only clippings I have are sort of very old. First of all let me tell you two things. First of all, I didn't keep the clippings of the newspapers, secondly, I refused to be interviewed about it.

So, I wasn't interviewed about it, they simply took the story as they got it from anyone. But the only clippings I happen to have, which I could dig up for you, are the ones from the newspapers in Italy, because it was sent to me by the South African embassy. That's why I've got them.

Julie Frederikse: Why on earth did they send them to you?

Albert Nolan: I don't know. Perhaps to tell me they knew all about it.

Julie Frederikse: And they are in Italian?

Albert Nolan: Yes.

Julie Frederikse: And would anybody have them?

Albert Nolan: I have them, those. But the rest of them I doubt whether anyone's kept all that—at least I don't know.

Julie Frederikse: OK. Well, maybe I might follow up to ask about those. When you said the job that I have to go back and do in South Africa, you're still clear about that?

Albert Nolan: Hm, yes very clear about that. I'm clear about it in my own mind, but it's difficult to find the right words to describe it to someone. Because I would describe it as doing theology.

But that doesn't sound particularly exciting or very important for the struggle in South Africa etc, but I believe it is.

So, you could say that at one level I came back to continue in the struggle as a Christian, as a priest, but the specific role, the specific contribution l feel I can make, is in the area of theology.

There are plenty of other people who could also do that, but are few people as convinced of the importance of that as I am. Frank Chikane is just as an example, that is why we work together.

But, you won't find very many others who are totally convinced that theology has an extremely important role to play.

And what I described to our General Chapter was, you see, [that] we are Dominicans and one of our specialities as Dominicans has always been theology. And I live in a country where theology is actually being used to promote the system. The way in which Christianity is associated with Apartheid or just generally with the system end where opposition to it is regarded as atheistic, a communist.

Now, that presents us with a particular theological problem that is different from most other countries where there is forms of oppression. There are some similarities in Latin America, but they haven't used Christianity and theology as obviously and intentionally as the South African regime has done throughout the ages, with the Dutch Reformed Church say behind it in that kind of thing.

And we're at a stage now where the opposition does come from the church. There are enormous problems about that, because the church is often hamstrung and not able to, as I said earlier, not able to get fully involved in the struggle. It hesitates at certain points and all the rest, because its theology doesn't enable them to do so. Whichever way you look at it, there is a very serious theological problem.

There is the problem, if you like, of the theory of what Christianity is. And this is very, very—how should I say—has an enormous influence because you're not merely talking about political theory or social theory or the theory that takes the form of policies etc. You are talking about a problem that affects the conscience of people.

What they feel guilty about, or not guilty about. You talk about something that's sacred for people or has a particularly strong influence on the way they will act or not act.

Talking about the way they understand God, and what God wants and what God will do to them. Now, all of that, whichever way you understand it, whether you understand it that God wants the system the way it is or whether you understand that God doesn't want it the way it is, is a very powerful social force.

And when that's all confused and mixed up, and all the rest, you are not easily going to move, how should I say, from where we are to something better. You might be able to do that, but you would do it with a great deal of confusion. And we wouldn't be quite sure that what we move to is all that much better, with that kind of confusion.

Because we are to a very large extent a so-called Christian country and religion and Christianity still plays a very important role in the lives of the people and so it is important what kind of Christianity it's going to be.

So, that's what I came back to contribute towards it. And I feel that's very important and since I know I can do that, and I am so convinced that it's important to do that, so I feel I have a role, a contribution.

Julie Frederikse: Since you're a person that really appreciates the concrete, the name of this institute sounds a bit vague to me—what would you say you do? What do you do? You've told me what your goals are, and what you want, but can you tell me more?

Albert Nolan: OK. The words 'Institute of Contextual Theology' all sound very abstract and that's true. Let's take theology to start off with.

Now, although that's an abstract word and not generally a people's word, it seems to us very clear that theology is something that has been confined to seminaries, universities, academic circles. Often generally clerical circles, middle class, etc.

Now, that's been its context to now, the context in which it happens. Now, we feel that should not be the case. Theology should happen and be done by the people at grass roots. In groups—youth groups, women's groups, and whatever other groups there are and within the struggle and from the experience of the struggle.

So, we use a word like theology because we don't want it to be simply confined to the context of people who generally side with the oppressors. And in a certain sense, reappropriate, get the people to reappropriate it for themselves.

If I use another word than theology you might understand me better. But the Bible is now possessed by the people who are on the whole on the side of the oppressor and they are the ones who use it, just in the same way they use the media or they use culture or they use education to perpetuate the system.

Now all of these things have to be taken out of their hands. It's not only weapons that have to be taken out of their hands, but the Bible has to be taken out of their hands, and given back to the people to whom it belongs.

Because the Bible of all things belongs to the poor, it's a book about the religion of the poor and the oppressed, the slaves in Egypt right the way through. Part of what we want to do is take the Bible and theology and give it back to the people.

Now, it's called contextual theology because we are aware of the fact that all theology comes from a particular context and we want a theology that develops from our context in South Africa, that is thoroughly South African, that comes from the grass roots, from the struggle, from the conflicts, from the people.

Now we're trying to enable that to happen. So, we're an institute because we're a group of people in an office with a steering committee, with a membership and all the rest who are trying to enable something to happen in South Africa.

So we have projects, but we don't try to possess them, we try to get them off the ground, initiate them let them go. I'll give you some examples

There were feminists, there were women around the country who were also interested in theology and what this had to do with the Bible. They didn't know one another, or there were no links or anything like that, so [we] brought them together, had conferences, enabled them to discuss this further, set up groups, write a book etc, etc.

So, we enable it to happen, but we don't possess it. Black theology to a large extent died out in South Africa. We enabled it to be revived. We organised conferences, again writing books, a reader on some short articles on black theology etc, etc. We revive it to enable it to go forward again an enabling job.

We work with the African Independent Churches. We are trying to help them to articulate their own theology. We are not trying to tell them what it ought to be, but their theology is contextual—it comes right out of the context of townships and of an African culture and of the experience of the moment and this is the way they understand what Christianity is about.

It's never articulated as a theology, it's never articulated in concepts, or systematically. So, we're helping it do that, so that they can say it to others, so that they can be in dialogue with others.

So, it's an enabling job. We're enabling something contextual to happen. And so forth and so forth.

We have all sorts of other groups that we work with where we can try to enable things to happen, try to publish what happens, try to fertilise the various things that do happen, provide people with information so that they can do their own theologising, and our hope is that out of that a South African theology will come.

Julie Frederikse: There is much said and written about white people and Apartheid. Can you actually situate for me this? Do you ever think about what am I doing as a white in the situation? Do you think it's relevant that you are a white? Can you say anything about your role as a white?

Albert Nolan: Well, first of all I believe in non-racialism if that's the way to express it. I would like to say that although the form the expression has taken is obviously a black/white thing, that [is] below and behind that. Very simply, the exploitation of people—there are oppressors and oppressed and that if one could even conceivably do away with race, and a class system could continue in which there are still poor people suffering, to get back to the beginning that the starting point is the suffering of people.

Whether those people are black or white is irrelevant, the people suffer. And if the people suffer who make them suffer are black or white is also irrelevant. At the present moment it is white, from my point of view you will still have a problem.

So that even if you have a kind of equality among the races, but no equality among the races, but no equality among rich and poor because there's unequal distribution of wealth, you just have the same problem in another form.

Now, because of that, the issue for me is oppressor and oppressed, not simply black or white, although I know only too well that it takes that form in South Africa and the myth of race has been used as a very effective way of oppressing people in South Africa.

Now, because of that, there's no problem for me. I don't feel guilty about that or I don't wish I were not a white South African like any other South African. We South Africans are of different shades of colour and racial backgrounds and national background as and all the rest.

A really important choice is between justice and injustice, oppressor end oppressed and that's the important thing, whether you make the choice or not. Now perhaps' through no fault of their own, there are many people who are oppressed, who haven't made an option for themselves if you know what I mean.

Perhaps I could just start using that term. We talk about an option for the poor, which might describe what I'm trying to do and describe what Latin American theologians and others are trying to do.

Make an option for the poor. Now, if you use that terminology, the issue is who's taking an option for the poor and who hasn't. And maybe the poor themselves are not taking the option for themselves, and for their cause, but either go along with things as it is and haven't been conscientised because they have a kind of faith in a religion which seems to think you couldn't possibly take an option for the cause of the poor themselves as God's cause.

But, there're also people who grew up on the other side, as not part of the oppressed, who can take an option for the oppressed and be one with them in the interests, concerns and in striving for justice.

And that that happens is very, very important. It happens everywhere. It could happen in Latin America, the Philippines, or anywhere else as well. But it's more remarkable in a way, or more stands out in South Africa, because of the colour.

You see, even if a person who is white takes an option for people who are black is much more of an anomaly than a Philippino who grew up in a middle class should take an option for the poor, it is hardly noticed, whereas the colour of our skin makes us conspicuous.

But in itself it's not a strange phenomenon. But anywhere in the world in any of the changes or revolutions or anything, there were certainly lots of middle class people who took an option for the poor, however you want to put it.

And that's happening here. So, I don't find it extraordinary, I don't find it odd, etc.

Because of the racial form of the oppression in South Africa, it's sometimes limiting—there's certain things because you're white, you wouldn't do, but you would let a black person do. But that's important not only in colour but in all sorts of other things.

If I haven't got a talent to do a particular thing and someone else has, I must let the other person do it and not try and push myself into it, so that's all part of my own philosophy anyway.

So, it doesn't bother me as a white that there's certain things I wouldn't be able to do. I couldn't easily write articles about black theology for example, or say that I'm writing about black experience.

I can't write from a black experience, but that alright, it doesn't have to be a problem. l can do other things.

Julie Frederikse: I would love to ask you a whole lot of questions, but can you just tell me about YCS[2] and YCW[3] and the action movement, in the context of the issue I'm asking you about, being white? What you said about encouraging people to take the option for the poor, was that one of the contributions of YCW?

Cos I understand you were part of the YCS . . .

Albert Nolan: Of [course], yes, not YCW. YCW has existed since shortly after the Second World War, in South Africa, and I was working with Catholic university students and went to Latin America, one of the things we learnt about is first actually the methods of the YCS—a method which YCW also used.

And so I introduced that method and eventually YCS into Catholic university, circles in South Africa, with the help of YCW from their experience and then into schools.

Now, when say l did it, I mean I was among people who did it, I wasn't alone. I did it with the students to a very large extent. So, I was National chaplain to YCS for about eight years or something like that, and certainly had a lot to do with the building up of YCS in South Africa.

CAM[4] was first of all YCS post-graduates after school or after university and then gradually broadened out to include people who hadn't been in YCS as well. And it's a small group [of] people and it's centred around Johannesburg—it's a movement of the type that's quite common int the Catholic Church that uses Review of Life, which is the See-Judge-Act and that's what all of those have in common.

It's a method of involvement in the struggle that characterises those three.

YCW working with workers, YCS with students and CAM being for adults. In this particular case, mostly white adults. We might have another group working in Soweto with adults.

---

2. Editorial Note: Young Christian Students.
3. Editorial Note: Young Christian Workers.
4. Editorial Note: The Christian Action Movement (CAM) was set up in the first half of the 1980s in Johannesburg, by people who had been involved in university YCS, and some who were not ever in YCS but were part of review groups of post-university people. Many of these were graduates who had participated in NCFS (National Catholic Federation of Students) and YCS and lived in Christian simple-lifestyle communities, characterised by shared values and activism, collective decision-making, sharing of chores and in some communities, sharing of money and resources.

Julie Frederikse: OK. So much of what you've been saying has been abstract or has been in theory and I'm just worried that someone will read this and might have trouble envisioning what these people actually do. So, can you give me some sense more experiential, anecdotal? I was going to ask you what achievement can you point out, but can you say that in concreter terms, can you tell me about some activity of YCS or something you've been involved in and you think 'this is whites working in'? Something you're really proud and pleased of this achievement that they did this and this?

Albert Nolan: Sure. I would hesitate to want to mention names if that doesn't bother you.

I'll come to actions in a moment. But the most important achievement of it is the building of leadership, and a good number of black and white leaders in the struggle have come out of YCS. The experience that they went through and all that has made them leaders and they're all over the place.

So as formation as leadership training, that's the path if you want to say it where I feel most pleased about that, it was really worthwhile, etc the number of leaders who have come out of that. OK? And that's black and white.

As regards actions, well they vary enormously. It's basically let's say putting right something that's wrong. And as I understand what justice is about in the Bible, there's a verb that's difficult to translate into English and the closest translation would be to do justice or put right or to wrong someone. To put right what is wrong.

Julie Frederikse: What is the verb?

Albert Nolan: I've forgotten what it is in Hebrew; if you can imagine it as a Hebrew word for justice, now that noun can be used as a verb. You haven't got a verb that corresponds to justice, we have to say to *do* justice, if you understand what I mean.

That doesn't help very much either. We talk about doing justice to a meal or something like that, but what I wanted to say is the closest you could get to the idea is to put right something that's wrong.

I wanted to say that, because that's a broad understanding of what work for justice means. Putting right what is wrong.

All the actions of YCS and CAM etc are always actions to try and put right something that's wrong. So, it could be anything from a bad geography teacher who doesn't teach geography well, is boring or something like that and then they work out how can we put right what is wrong here.

It could be a drunken teacher or it could be something that happened in the church, or it could be something in the community or it could be problems that kids are having with their parents.

And of course you don't just jump to conclusions about what is wrong that has to be put right. You have a longer view of 'what is wrong' and 'am I to blame perhaps' or 'is it really wrong' etc and what do you do about putting it right?

But it could be what appear to be tiny little things, it could be big things, you get involved in. You might find something else is going on which in your judgement from [a] Christian point of view is a process of putting right something in the schools say, or in the system then you would join it.

But, the simplest way I can say it is if I say actions, which is the word generally used, then people think of marches on the streets or something else like that, which is not what I have in mind.

An action could be talking to somebody. But what is characteristic of it is that it's a putting right something that is wrong.

Now, very often the young people do very small actions of that sort. As I say, there's something wrong with the way geography is taught, and everybody's always failing so they do something about it and put that right.

Now those are the things that build leadership. It is the fact that hundreds of times, you have done that, you've taken the initiative, you've involved other people in doing it, you found a way of doing it, when it didn't work you reviewed why it didn't work and again that's the stuff of which leaders are made. That's education.

And we're involved in that kind of education and out of that leaders have come. So, what am I saying? I'm saying I'm most pleased that there's leaders coming out of it and they came out of it through little actions that were reflected upon continuously.

Julie Frederikse: Do you have any visions of ·the future of South Africa that you are working towards? And do you ever look at the news one day and think what's happening and think we're closer to it? I know that's the question that nobody want to answer—but do you have any sense?

Albert Nolan: Oh, yeah. One of the things about church or religion is that we don't have a political policy in any way or a blueprint for the future, but we do have a vison I think of our own . . . religion provides for the vision of a just society, where there would therefore be peace.

And in a South African context, there's no doubt about it, it would have to be—I won't go into all the reasons why, but it would have to be a democratic society, one person, one vote, and to me nothing short of that is ever going to bring peace.

It has to be a non-racial society and not a multi-racial society where you've still got groups where their interests balance out against one another in some formular or other that's again not going to bring peace, but that's non-racial, so that race is as irrelevant as creed or gender or anything else.

It has to include redistribution of wealth in some form or another, because if you still have rich and poor, even if it's a democratic society, even if it's non-racial etc, it's still oppressive and it wouldn't be just, so it would have to be one that redistributes the wealth in some way or another.

And obviously common citizenship, common patriotism, one nation, that sort of thing sems to me to be the things that are necessary.

I would think the problem comes with sustaining that. How do you build a sustainable society. In that area it is your culture - how do you have a new South African culture, and within that you have the issue of what role is religion going to play? In sustaining this, in making sure that people's values continue to be the values in community and quality and you could even change structures.

You could have people continually trying to jeopardise those structures for selfish reasons, but it's how you contain that and sustain that new system—and we're assuming it's changed—which is the area where I think religion has a role to play.

Julie Frederikse: When were you born?

Albert Nolan: 1934 . . . 51 this year.

Julie Frederikse: So, I'm just comparing the situation now with the forming of JODAC[5] and the Congress of Democrats (COD)[6] in the

---

5. Editorial Note: Johannesburg Democratic Action Committee was an affiliate of the United Democratic Front (UDF) and gathered white activists in Johannesburg. It was formed as an affiliate of the UDF in 1983 and provided an opportunity for whites to join the struggle against Apartheid.
6. Editorial Note: The South African Congress of Democrats (SACOD) was a radical left-wing white, anti-Apartheid organisation founded in South Africa in 1952 or 1953 as part of the multi-racial Congress Alliance, after the African National Congress (ANC) invited whites to become part of the Congress Movement.

fifties. Do you have any remembrance of those times? Do you remember what your reaction was then to the COD movement as compared to how you feel now about JODAC?

Albert Nolan: Well, what I do remember is Trevor Huddlestone.[7] I didn't meet him, but we always read about him in the papers and then he wrote the book *Nought for your Comfort* which was when I was training to be a priest at that time a very important book for us.

[I] Remember I came from the Cape—a lot of these things like COD was a Transvaal Johannesburg type of thing. So, I wasn't' directly involved in anything. I was younger then I suppose and not particularly involved in those things.

Ok, I do remember admiring Trevor Huddlestone very much. I do remember feeling that one would want to side with him—that's about as close as I got to doing anything. I didn't understand a great deal of what was going on, but by that stage, I would decidedly be against the government, but without a clear idea of what 1955 meant for example, what the freedom charter was really all about as I would know it now.

Julie Frederikse: I was going to ask you about the risk of getting involved as individuals—the heroes and figures one would admire, would there have been others besides Trevor Huddlestone?

Albert Nolan: Not really. Trevor Huddleston definitely stands out as a hero for me. No, I can't say that there's any other particular one. I mean later on perhaps someone like Mandela could—became a hero figure, but that was much, much later on.

No, I don't think I could safely say anyone else. Probably hero figures in other parts of the world, because when you're a Catholic in an international religion and an international order like Dominicans, there were other parts of the world one admired.

An in my particular case, the particular things I was interested in was theology and they would have been theologians and then admiration for many of the Latin American and the things that they were doing.

---

7. Editorial Note: Ernest Urban Trevor Huddleston CR KCMG (15 June 1913–20 April 1998) was an English Anglican bishop. He was the Bishop of Stepney in London before becoming the second Archbishop of the Church of the Province of the Indian Ocean. He was best known for his anti-Apartheid activism and his book *Naught for Your Comfort*.

So, often enough my attention in terms of ideals and heroes was outside of the country rather than inside.

But Trevor Huddlestone I remember particularly from South Africa.

Julie Frederikse: Energies. Where do you channel them now? Are you involved in any political organisations?

Albert Nolan: Yes. I'm involved in JODAC.

Julie Frederikse: Why?

Albert Nolan: Well, because I think at the moment it's extremely important to have extra-parliamentary activity—the parliamentary activity seems to me no way out—you're not going to get anywhere via the parliament.

It's a racial parliament, it's an undemocratic parliament and all the rest. So, if you want to build democracy and racialism and things like that, then you must—it has to start outside parliament. It has to be extra parliamentary.

I would think that whatever one was part of should be affiliated to WDF[8], to be part of a complete front. I can see the importance of working in different constituencies, like students, women, but also white, Indian, coloured etc. Not that one wants any of those divisions, but there are.

So, it would be natural for me to work in the white constituencies of Johannesburg. I've worked most of my life with blacks, but still should work in the white constituency, because that's where I belong.

What other reasons would I want to be part of JODAC? Well, it's exciting building something like this at this time. For years we've agonised over the fact that there was nothing like that, and the white left was not at all organised. So, that's why I'm there.

I do also a lot of work with CAM of course. And the actions of CAM are generally, to very large extent anyway, in the church. They often have activities outside of that.

Individuals themselves can have activities, because CAM itself is a review of life based thing. We review what we are involved in. But everybody's an activist of one kind or another, and very often an activist in the church, trying to change things in the church, develop things in the church etc.

---

8. Editorial Note: Women Development Foundation.

So, a lot of my time is spent with that. And then of course, I work with ICT and then I travel around giving talks lectures, I try to write and get things written and to find time for studying etc.

Julie Frederikse: I'm unclear. Really quickly, could you tell me—you said you worked for blacks before. Could you just again tell me . . .

Albert Nolan: O yes of course, I didn't give you the racial composition of things.

YCS started as white university students but then it gradually became mixed and when we went into high schools it was majority black, so 90% of YCS was black. So, one of the features of YCS was one of the first, apart from the movements that are in exile, etc the first thoroughly non-racial movement that actually mixed people in the same movement, in the same committees. So, it could be a white or a black who was president or coordinator any particular year.

Julie Frederikse: First, what year was that, that you were doing it?

Albert Nolan: 1977. But we really became mixed in about 1977. But you see, how can I describe what I'm trying to say? I mean usually they are thoroughly non-racial. But there was nothing like the UDF at that stage.

Earlier on of course, there had been the ANC and the Congress of Democrats etc, etc which had been mixed.

The black consciousness period, when everything was divided—even though everyone agreed with each other they were nevertheless separated—we started something where they were together and sort of worked through the problems of that and I think very successfully. That's a small group of people.

It was an experiment in non-racialism all right. That, and even in what l call Parish work that I have done, I worked in Stellenbosch in the so called coloured community,

So, I'd been mixing a year in the office at ICT, I mean I the only white, and I got to African Independent Churches. I've been to their conferences find I'm the only white among them.

When I went to their conference three weeks ago, I was the first white who had ever been to one of them. So, I'm often the only white in black circles, but then it comes to the actual politics, my constituency is white Johannesburg.

Julie Frederikse: How do you define actual politics?

Albert Nolan: Well, when I'm working with the African Independent Churches or something of those things, I'm working more directly as theology.

I'm trying to understand Christianity in relation to this context. I'm there in the capacity of someone who's supposed to be informed about that. It's a particular form of service, which I see as related to the struggle, definitely.

But when I mean JODAC, I'm not their theologian [and] I'm not their priest, I'm there as one member among others. I'm there working out about what do we do about Johannesburg liberals. How do we carry on this campaign? It's two very different roles.

The direct political one, which is more the JODAC one, it's very difficult for me to go and sit in a civic association in Soweto, in the middle of KOSAS or whatever else trade union, and try to just be one with them.

There's no point in fooling myself that I am. That's not my constituency.

Julie Frederikse: So, before JODAC, did you have a kind of gap?

Albert Nolan: Ja, you could say there was. There were often discussions and little things going on but I suppose you could say there was never the more direct political activity that's possible now with UDF.

I mean that wasn't possible for a lot of people, not only whites.

Julie Frederikse: As you have explained, you deal with the whites in JODAC. But do you ever deal with the white majority, the white groupings, the more conservative roles?

That's a criticism often, it's preaching to the converted.

Albert Nolan: Ah. Let me just say I've got a family of course, and I've got a family that's very conservative for that matter, politically. And therefore relatives and lots of friends and so forth. So I know those circles quite a bit. And then through the church, I spend a lot of time talking to liberals an even conservatives in church and workshops and things like that. And then through JODAC because they try to have public meetings, which does include them when I gave a talk the other night, to a broad public JODAC meeting, which was very much a matter of talking to liberals etc, etc. PFP[9] types. So ja, I do have some contact with them. Not a great deal and do work to some extent with them. As I said earlier, I'm very interested in how people take that step. And whether they take it, because as you said, they can get stuck there.

Julie Frederikse: Have you seen JODAC help people take that step?

Albert Nolan: Yes. Precisely because JODAC has provided a platform on which to step. Because if you take the step now by say, moving from being a member of the PFP Youth Croup or something else like that, to being a member of JODAC, you've got an actual concrete way of taking the step. That helps.

And then through its own argument that extra-parliamentary politics is a good thing, it is not illegal and is not banned and you don't have to go underground and you don't have to be chased by security police, etc by being extremely parliamentary. So, by the whole creating of that possibility and argument for it, I think has made the step possible for people for whom it might not have been possible before.

---

9. Editorial Note: The Progressive Party (Afrikaans: *Progressiewe Party*) was a liberal party in South Africa which, during the era of Apartheid, was considered the left-wing of the all-white parliament. The party represented the legal opposition to Apartheid within South Africa's white minority. It opposed the ruling National Party's racial policies, and championed the rule of law.

Cardijn Studies: On the Church in the World of Today: Volume 4/2 2023

3
Kairos Theology[1]

Kairos theology is the name we give to the type of theology which was first committed to writing in a well-known document signed by more than 150 church persons and published in South Africa on 25 September 1985. It was entitled *The Kairos Document: Challenge to the Church: A Theological Comment on the Political Crisis in South Africa.* Very seldom, if ever, in the history of South Africa had a theological statement made such an impact upon the country—its churches, its politicians and its people. Never before had so many people in South Africa been caught up in a theological controversy, for the document was thought of as indeed very controversial.

Nor was the impact of the *Kairos Document* limited to South Africa. It was read and discussed in many parts of the world and gave rise to Kairos groups in several countries, as well as other Kairos documents (for example, in Central America) and a seven-nation document known as *The Road to Damascus: Kairos and Conversion.*

While the idea of a Kairos theology originated in South Africa and whole articles on this kind of theology can be found in numerous Journals, the only book that explores the different expressions of Kairos theology was edited in Nicaragua and published in Spanish, *El Kairos en Centroamenca.* It has not been translated into English.

Our study of Kairos theology in this chapter will be based almost exclusively upon the original South African document of September 1985.

---

1. Taken from *Doing Theology in Context: South African Perspectives*, edited by John W de Gruchy and Charles Villa-Vicencio (Cape Town/New York: David Philip/ Orbis, 1994), 212–218.

The Story Behind the Document

The *Kairos Document* was an initiative of the Institute for Contextual Theology (ICT) in Johannesburg. However, it was not planned or even foreseen by the staff of ICT. It simply happened as a result of ICT's method of doing theology.

The Institute does not teach theology; it simply enables people to do their own theological reflection upon their own praxis and experience. The staff of ICT are active in bringing Christians together, facilitating discussion and action, recording what people say, and doing whatever research may be required to support the reflections, arguments and actions of the people.

It was in pursuance of this method that two staff members brought together a group of about ten interested parties in Soweto one Saturday morning in 1985 to reflect upon South Africa's latest crisis, the recently declared State of Emergency. As usual, it was thought that this meeting might lead to a plan action which might involve some more Christians. Nobody was thinking about a theological document or anything like that.

The meeting was more animated and fruitful than usual. More meetings were held. More and more people were involved. The staff were given assignments to do, like biblical research into the meaning of Chapter 13 of the letter to the Romans and historical research into the Christian tradition on violence and tyranny. Minutes were taken at these meetings, and the insights of the participation and research done by the staff and others were collated into a document. That was amended again and again with a view to the publication of a pamphlet, when someone suggested that it should become a document or a statement signed by the participants, as well as others from around the country, as a challenge to the churches 'from below'.

And that indeed is what it became: theology from below. The seriousness of the crisis, together with the anger and frustration of the people, motivated the participants to seek out what they believed and what they did not believe. The Institute as a facilitating body rather than an authoritative body recorded what the participants said without any censorship or amendment. All the participants became what we later called 'the Kairos theologians'.

A Contextual Theology

Contextual theology is the kind of theology which reflects, explicitly and consciously, upon its context in the light of the gospel of Jesus Christ. In other words, it deals with the problems, the issues and the questions that arise for a Christian in any particular context and especially in a context of oppression and suffering.

The *Kairos Document* was vividly and dramatically contextual, it came straight out of the flames of the townships in 1985. Those who had not experienced the oppression, the repression, the sufferings and the struggles of the people of the townships at that same time were not able to understand the faith questions that were being tackled here, let alone the answers. What were these questions and concerns?

The first question or concern was about the intolerable suffering of the people at the time. In their meetings and discussions, the theologians, priests, ministers and other church workers who came to be known as the Kairos theologians related one horror story after another about what the police and the army were doing to people in the townships. Most of these Kairos theologians were quite ordinary pastors, and many of them had never been involved in anything that might be called 'political'. They were simply horrified by what they had seen with their own eyes, and they came to the meetings with the smell of teargas still in their nostrils. They came with very serious and urgent faith questions. Where was God in all of this? What did God want his ministers to do in this crisis? What could they do or say to stop the violence, the violence of the aggressor?

It is ironical that the Kairos Document should subsequently have been accused of promoting violence and even murder. Or perhaps this is just another indication of the very different perceptions of what was happening in the townships and of who was responsible for the violence.

The second concern was that all of this was being done in the name of Christianity. The Bible (especially Romans 13) was being used to justify the actions of the State. This gave rise to urgent questions about the 'Christianity' of the State and about the way in which it used the Bible. As minsters of the Word of God, the Kairos theologians felt that they simply had to contradict this 'State Theology'—as strongly and as unequivocally as possible. People had to know that this was not Christianity, but in fact, the very opposite of all that we mean by Christianity.

A third concern was the ineffectiveness of the official church response to Apartheid and, even more so, to the crisis created by the State of Emergency. Official church statements were not only too mild and too vague but they were simply not bringing the full power and challenge of the gospel of Jesus Christ to bear upon the actual situation There was no wish to be disloyal to the churches or to embarrass church leaders. The question that arose out of the realities of this socio-historical context was: How can we enable the gospel to come across powerfully and effectively to all the people in these times?

Clearly linked to this was the concern about the dangerous temptation of neutrality or sitting on the fence. We had all seen or experienced the temptation to remain on the side-lines and to argue that the problems were political and therefore none of our business or, at least, that the church must never take sides but offer the people some kind of 'third way'. The very serious concern of the Kairos theologians was that we might be tempted to betray the gospel and to betray the suffering people of the townships by our neutrality. Was it not our neutrality, among other things, that had enabled this oppressive system to continue for so long and to reach the brutality and fierceness of the repression of the 1980s? How could we possibly not take sides against such evil, injustice and cruelty? And what does reconciliation and forgiveness mean in such circumstances? These were serious theological questions.

Another concern that gave rise to some real searching questions was the crisis in the church itself. The church itself was divided. There was now a white church and a black church even within the same denominations. The two no longer understood the implications of their Christian faith in the same way. Both the oppressor and the oppressed had allegiance to the same Christ, the same beliefs and the same church. That was a really serious crisis for Christianity. Some of the participants were asking whether in such circumstances Christianity had not become so ambiguous that it no longer had any meaning at all.

One of the greatest concerns of the Kairos theologians was that the church had not been the bearer of hope in our society. It had criticised, it had blamed, it had been cautious and careful but it had not preached the bold and prophetic Christian message of hope. It was felt that the Christian message of hope was being neglected and overlooked precisely at a time when almost everyone in South Africa was desperately in need of hope for the future. But just how does one preach hope in such circumstances?

Last but not least, it was strongly felt that the time for talking was over. What was needed and what the people were crying out for was action. The church was being accused of discussing, debating, preaching and making statements, but not acting. This gave rise to the very important question. What action must the church, as church, take in these circumstances?

We see then, how this particular socio-historical context of oppression gave rise to numerous theological questions. We can also see that although questions have some similarity to the questions asked by people in other contexts of oppression, these were decidedly the questions arising out of the context of South Africa in 1985.

A Theology of Liberation

Kairo theology has much in common with liberation theology. In fact it might well be described as a species or type of liberation theology. Like other theologies of liberation, it makes use of social analysis and is driven by Christian faith-based struggle for the liberation of the oppressed.

Social analysis permeates every page of the *Kairos Document*. One section of the document is entitled 'Social Analysis', but the process of analysis and references to social analysis and its importance can be found throughout the document.

The social analysis of the *Kairos Document* was simply the commonly held analysis of black people in South Africa, namely that our society was racist, divided into white and black and that structurally the whites were oppressors and blacks were the oppressed. This was not a matter of accusing all whites or excusing all blacks. Some whites might be on the side of the oppressed and some blacks might be themselves oppressors, as in the homelands. But a social analysis of the structure of our society reveals a power relationship of oppressor and oppressed just as it does in Latin America, and many other countries.

Kairos theology, like all other theologies of liberation, has no difficulty with an analysis of society into oppressor and oppressed because it is exactly the same analysis we find throughout the Bible. The *Kairos Document* is at pains to point out the Bible says about the oppressor and about the oppressed—and therefore about the liberation of the oppressed. But the analysis of the *Kairos Document* goes one step further. The South African government is not only oppressive, it is altogether illegitimate, and at that moment (1985) it had become tyrannical. According to the Kairos theologians, a tyrannical regime has no moral legitimacy and has become the enemy of God.

One sees how closely related social analysis and theological reflection are. And yet theology must go one step further in order to qualify as a genuine Kairos theology. It must analyse and reflect upon a particular *kairos* or critical moment of history.

Kairos theology does not only do social analysis of the general situation, it does conjunctural analysis, or analysis of the particular crisis at that point in time because of the conjuncture, or meeting, of oppressing forces. The crisis in 1985 was brought about by, on the one side, tyrannical repression (detentions, trials, killings, torture, bannings, propaganda, states of emergency) and on the other side, all-out resistance (boycotts, strikes, uprisings, burnings, armed struggles). This was the *kairos* at that time.

A Prophetic Theology

A prophetic theology is one that begins by reading the signs of the times. This is done not only by means of a social analysis of the times, but also by interpreting the times from God's point of view. Thus, a particular point in time can be seen as a visitation from God, a warning, an opportunity, a promise, a punishment, a reward or a call to conversion. Theological interpretation here means discerning what kind of time we are living in and what God is saying to us at this particular moment of time.

Prophecy, or prophetic theology, always includes, implicitly or explicitly, a call to conversion, or *metanoia*. And this call is generally preceded by a warning about what terrible consequences or punishments will ensue if there is no repentance and conversion. On the other hand there is also the prophetic promise of rewards and blessings in the future if there is a change of heart, or *metanoia*.

Kairos theology is really just another name for prophetic theology. The *Kairos Document* describes what it is trying to do as prophetic theology. In other words the Kairos theology of the *Kairos Document* was simply the explicit revival of doing theology in a prophetic mode with a strong emphasis upon the reading of the signs of the times at a very particular time, or *kairos*, in the history of church and society in South Africa.

Kairos is a Greek word which is used in the Bible to refer to 'a moment of truth', 'a crisis that is shaking the foundations', 'a moment of grace and opportunity, a favourable time in which God issues a challenge to decisive action'. This is how the *Kairos Document* interpreted the crisis of 1985 in South Africa. It goes on to say, 'It is a dangerous time because, if this opportunity is missed, and allowed to pass by, the loss for the church, for the gospel and for all the people of South Africa will be immeasurable'.

One recognises the prophetic warning here, which is then underlined in the document by the quotation from Luke 19:44, where the word *kairos* is actually used in the Greek text. The reference to this time as 'a moment of grace and opportunity' constitutes the prophetic promise that this *kairos* holds out for the future of South Africa—for church and society. The statement that God is issuing 'a challenge to decisive action' is of course the call to conversion and action.

The essence of Kairos theology is the act of interpreting a particular crisis as a *kairos* in the biblical sense of an encounter with God, who is speaking to us now with warnings, promise and a call to action. It is an act of reading the signs of the times. It is a reflection upon a faith experience rather than an intellectual conclusion drawn from biblical texts and principles.

So, all more important is the recognition that when we read the signs of the times or interpret our *kairos*, we are saying something about the future. Prophetic theology is concerned not only about the present but also about the future. In fact prophetic theology can see the future, or various possible futures, in the present crisis. It can predict future catastrophes if nothing is done now, and it can promise great blessings if the present opportunity is taken seriously.

In the Greek words of our theological tradition, the present moment of truth and decision is our *kairos* and the future catastrophe or blessing is our *eschaton*. In practice, what this means is that prophetic theology, and therefore Kairos theology, should always be, in the final analysis, a theology of hope.

The *Kairos Document* is in the end a message of hope, and the section (4.6) should be noted and emphasised. The hopefulness of this kind of theology is sometimes overlooked because of the powerfully critical stance that the document takes towards the *status quo* of church and government. The theology of government and dominant white majority, the theology of the oppressor, is called State Theology and is condemned in no uncertain terms. It is associated with the devil and the Antichrist.

Not only that, even the usual unprophetic theology of the church is criticised. The Kairos theologians were unanimous in their criticism of church statements and abstract generalisations They began to label this as 'Church Theology'.

Like all prophets, the Kairos theologians were critical of the present and also about the future. Like all prophets they were also very emotional about the times of the present. Feelings of anger and frustration, condemnations and terms of clear-cut distinctions between good and evil, God and the devil, are characteristic of the *Kairos Document*. One of the criticisms of the document at the time was that it was too emotional.

When you think about it, this is an accusation that could have been levelled against any of the great biblical prophets. They were all very emotional, but it was their strength. One of the things that made the *Kairos Document* so powerful (and so controversial) was the feelings that pervaded its message. There is, of course, no other way of doing prophetic theology.

Perhaps there is one difference between Kairos theology and what is generally thought of as prophetic theology. Kairos theology is a community theology. It is not the theology of an individual but the reflections and feelings of groups of Christians at a particular time in a particular circumstance. Prophetic theology generally associated with an individual prophet or an individual writer producing a document. Signed by 153 Christians, Kairos theology initiated a process of democratising theology itself.

Assessment

Despite its obvious value and importance, Kairos theology has its limitations. Theology and theological reflection must cover a far larger area of issues and concerns than only social and political crisis. There are matters of permanent concern like sin, values, God, creation, Jesus Christ, salvation, the environment and so forth. And there are more personal concerns like relationships, prayer and death that any comprehensive theology would have to deal with that Kairos theology could never claim to be a complete and comprehensive theology.

There are also very serious limitations with regard to the practice of Kairos theology. Very few people today are *doing* Kairos theology, and nothing much is being written in this prophetic mode. South

Africa faces even more serious crises today than it did in 1985, but there is very little theological reflection upon our present *kairos* as our moment of truth. A few years ago, ICT published a pamphlet about 'the violence'. They called it the 'New *Kairos*'. But this line of thought has not generated much interest.

In 1989, Christians from seven third-world countries co-operated in a venture that has been called the International Kairos. A document entitled *The Road to Damascus and Conversion* was signed by hundreds of Christians in South Africa, Namibia, South Korea, the Philippines, El Salvador, Nicaragua and Guatemala. The document issued a prophetic call to conversion addressed to all Christians who are associated with the oppression of the poor and the indigenous people of the third world. It caused a stir at the time, but the initiative was not followed up, and it is difficult to assess how much this kind of Kairos theology still influences the thinking and the actions of Christians in the world today. Perhaps that in itself is part of our present crisis.

Cardijn Studies: On the Church in the World of Today: Volume 4/2 2023

4
The Eschatology of the Kairos Document[1]

The eschatology of the *Kairos Document* is implicit. Nowhere is it spelt out as an eschatology and I do not think that those who were responsible for the document were consciously making use of any particular eschatological framework. However, the use that is made of the *kairos* idea and the proclamation of our present crisis in South Africa as a divine *kairos* has far-reaching implications for eschatology.

Let me try and unpack the understanding of eschatology that is, I believe, implicit in the *Kairos Document.* We begin with some account of the three kinds of time that are represented by the Greek words *chronos, kairos* and *eschaton.*

Chronos: Chronos means time as a measurement. It is the time of measured hours and dates, the time that is recorded on clocks and calendars. An historical epoch in this way of thinking is something that is identified by the date when it began and the date when it ended. It is what one might call quantified time. This is what comes to mind immediately when the word time is mentioned: a quantified measurement. However, this is not the way the Bible thinks of time.

Kairos: This word, on the other hand, reflects time as a quality. A particular *Kairos* is the particular quality or mood of an event. This is clearly and succinctly expressed in the famous passage from Ecclesiastes (3:1–8),

> There is a time for everything; a time for giving birth,
> a time for dying,
> a time for planting,

---

1. *Missionalia* 152 (August 1987): 285–92.

a time for uprooting,
a time for killing,
a time for healing,
a time for knocking down,
a time for building,
a time for tears,
a time for laughter,
a time for mourning,
a time for dancing,
a time for loving,
a time for hating,
a time for war,
a time for peace.

For the Hebrew, to know the time was not a matter of knowing the hour or the date, it was a matter of knowing what kind of time it was. Was it a time for tears, or a time for laughter, a time for war or a time for peace? To misjudge the time in which one was living might be disastrous. To continue to mourn and fast during a time of blessing would be like sowing during harvest time (see Zach 7:1-3). Time here is the quality or mood of events.

Meaningful to those Involved in the Struggle: This concept of time is not entirely foreign to us. It is particularly meaningful to those who inherit an African culture and even more meaningful when we are involved in an intensified struggle to change the times. We know about times of mourning that makes it inappropriate to celebrate a joyful Christmas. We have discussions about whether it is a time for boycotting or a time for returning to school. There is a time for conflict and confrontation and a time for reconciliation and peace.

Prophets Read the Signs of the Times: In the Bible, the prophet was someone who could tell the time. He (or she) could see what kind of time it was and what kind of action would be appropriate now. The prophets could read the signs of the times, which means they could interpret the *kairos*, interpret the signs that would indicate what kind of time it was (compare Mt 16:3 with Lk 12:56).

God Speaks through this Crisis: Prophecy, however, was not just a matter of knowing one's *kairos*; it was also a matter of finding God in it. For the prophets, God determined the different times and therefore it was God who speaks to us and challenges us through our particular *kairos*. Revelation has a tremendous immediacy here. God is directly involved in the changing times, God speaks loudly and clearly through this crisis or that conflict or some victory over the forces of evil.

A divine *Kairos*

This is not to say that every moment of chronological time is equally important or significant and that God can be found equally in every and any moment. Every event in history is not a *kairos*. A divine *kairos* is a very special and significant time. There are lulls in history when nothing of significance happens. For the Bible, such chronological times are simply not history. History is the succession of God-inspired events. The gift of the prophet is the ability to recognise such events, such critical times and to spell them out as moments of truth, as challenges, as opportunities, as times for decision and action. A *kairos* is a privileged time that not everyone is called to witness or participate in. Such was of course the time of Jesus and that is why he could say to his disciples: "Happy the eyes that see what you see, for I tell you that many prophets and kings wanted to see what you see and never saw it" (Lk 10:23–24). But even this is not all. The real specialness and seriousness of a prophetic *kairos* is determined by its relationship to another kind of time: the eschaton.

Eschaton

As the word itself indicates, the most important quality of this kind of time is its finality or ultimateness. It is the last time, the final, furthest, utmost or extreme time. The mistake here is to understand this finality in terms of measured chronological time. The finality of the *eschaton* is a quality that defines what kind of time it is, not a quantified measurement that puts it at the end of a long calendar of events. In fact, finality or ultimateness describes the relationship of some future event to a *kairos*. The *eschaton* is a future act of God that has finality for us because it determines the quality, the mood and seriousness of our present time, that is to say, it transforms the present moment into a particular kind of kairos.

But let us be more concrete

The Eschaton is a Future Event: In the first place, the eschaton is a future event. A very important characteristic of all prophetic thinking is that it turns the attention of the people from the past to the future. Prophets are called prophets precisely because they speak about the future. Instead of trying to understand the present in terms of events of the past (for example, Exodus, Mount Sinai or King David), the prophets ask the people to think of the present time in terms of a future act of God. They challenge the people to break with the past and to look forward to something new: 'Remember not the former things', says God in Isaiah, 'I am going to do a new thing' (43:18–19).

The *Eschaton* is a New Event: The *eschaton* is a qualitatively and radically new event. It is interesting to notice how often the prophets use the words 'new': the new covenant, the new age, a new heart, a new spirit, the new heaven and new earth, the new Jerusalem or simply the fact that God is going to do a new thing. They looked forward to a future in which new and unprecedented things would happen, and even when they looked back to the past and the traditions of the past, they would interpret them anew in view of the new future. Thus, the covenant makes them think of the new covenant to come, the exodus turns their attention to the new exodus and Jerusalem to the new Jerusalem and so forth.

The prophets did not use the Greek word *eschaton*. When they spoke of the new future they called it 'the day of Yahweh', 'the day of vengeance', 'the later days'. 'the days that are coming' or simply 'the day'. Jesus is making use of the same idea when he speaks of 'the coming of the kingdom of God'.

The New Future is Near at Hand: The first and most important thing that all prophets, including Jesus, have to say about this new future, or *eschaton*, is that it is 'near', 'at hand', 'coming soon'. The prophets stand up to make the momentous announcement that the 'day of Yahweh is near' (see for example Is 13:6,9; Jer 46:10; Ezek 7:7,12; 30:3; Joel 1:15; 4:14; Zeph 1:7,14; Zech 14:1) and Jesus comes to proclaim that 'the kingdom of God is near' (Mt 4:17 and par). Of course, they are not all referring to the same calendar day. The *eschaton* is a new saving act of God that was imminent or near for them at that time.

God Will Put Right What Is Wrong: The new saving act of God that will happen on the day of Yahweh is an act of judgment and salvation. God will punish those who are presently doing evil and save, vindicate or liberate those who are now enslaved or in exile or suffering oppression. The Hebrew verb 'to judge' means literally 'to put right what is wrong'. We can say then that the *eschaton* is an event of the near future in which God is going to put right all that is presently wrong. That will mean punishment for those who are doing wrong and salvation for those who are being wronged.

The Forces of Evil will be Destroyed: In the minds of the Old Testament prophets this future event will take the form of a mighty war in which the forces of evil will be destroyed so that peace and justice may reign on earth. Many of the prophets give vivid and terrifying descriptions of this mighty war of liberation. For but a few examples, one can read about the imminent destruction of Babylon and Edom in Isaiah 13 and 34 and the terrifying massacre of the Egyptians by the Babylonians in Jeremiah 46:1–24 and Ezek 30, not to mention the many descriptions of the slaughter of the Jewish ruling class in Jerusalem on the day of Yahweh because of all their sins (see for example Joel 2:1–11 and Ezek 37).

The prophets found no pleasure in describing all this horrific bloodshed. They trembled and shuddered at the very thought of it and they described the fear and suffering of so many of the people with great compassion. Theirs is not a dispassionate and objective description of a war, but a prophetic warning about a world-shaking event that will be experienced as a cosmic upheaval that changes the face of the earth and is a turning point in human history. It is an *eschaton*.

Peace is the Outcome: But the day of Yahweh is not only a day of vengeance, a time of gloom and doom. The prophets were in no doubt about the terrifying seriousness of what was going to happen, the awful seriousness of God's anger. But they never lost hope. On the contrary, the peace, the salvation, the justice and the equality that they were always hoping for would be the outcome of these very wars and upheavals. They have equally vivid descriptions of the peace and happiness that God will bring: when the lion lies down with the lamb (Isa 11:6-9, 65:25) and swords are melted into plough shares (Isa 2:2-5, Mic 4: 1-5), when there will be nothing more to fear (Zeph 3:13) and peace and justice will reign supreme (Isa 32:16-17) because the law will be written in the hearts of the people (Jer 31:33) and the spirit of God will be in them (Ezek 36:26). On that day, God will put right all that is now wrong. The oppressors will be destroyed or converted and the poor and oppressed will live in peace (Zeph 3).

This same idea of an *eschaton* appears in the New Testament when Jesus speaks about the coming of wars and rumours of wars (Mk 13) and the destruction of Jerusalem (Lk 19:43–44, 21:20–23, 23:28). This he speaks of as the birth pangs of God's kingdom (Mk 13).

A Moment of Grace: However, for Jesus and the prophets the destructive side of the *eschaton*, the bloodshed, is not inevitable. A *kairos* is a moment of grace, a unique opportunity precisely because the *eschaton* or day of reckoning is near. It is a time for decision and action, a time for oppressors and wrong-doers to be converted. And at the same time, the *kairos* is a time for rejoicing and for hope because the *eschaton* as the day of liberation is near at hand - whether the oppressor is converted or not, whether there will be bloodshed or not. The element of hopefulness and expectancy in any genuine kairos should not be overlooked. It is indeed one of the constitutive elements of a divine *kairos*, because you cannot have a *kairos* without an *eschaton*. The two are paralleled again and again in the Bible in statements like: The time has come, the end is near; the time has come, the day of Yahweh is near; the time is now, the kingdom is near; the kairos had come, the *eschaton* is near.

The *Eschaton* is Near: Here again we would need to be reminded that the nearness of an *eschaton* is not a matter of *chronos* or measured time. In other words, a prophet would not be able to tell you the day or the hour when all these things will happen. Jesus makes this quite clear when he says that nobody, not even he himself, knows the day or the hour (Mk 13:32 and par). But the impossibility of pinning the *eschaton* down to a chronological date did not make Jesus or the prophets any less certain about the central truth that their *eschaton* was near. What they are speaking about then, is another kind of time relationship, the extremely close relationship between the present *kairos* and a future *eschaton*.

If we believe that war, revolution, liberation or any other total upheaval is imminent, this will colour our whole understanding of our present reality. Once we realise that something totally new is about to happen, we are already living in a new time. Or if we come to believe that the day of reckoning is upon us, we are forced to decide, to make our choices and take sides immediately. It is the approaching *eschaton* that turns our present crisis into a make-or-break *kairos*.

Reading the Signs of the Times: That leaves us with the question of how one is to know that there is an *eschaton* on the horizon. The answer is quite simply that we discover this, as the prophets did, by reading the signs of the times. If one interprets one's own time correctly and especially if one can see the events of one's time with the eyes of God, then one sees clearly what all the signs are pointing to. One can foresee what is going to happen sometime in the near future, even if one cannot calculate the exact day or the hour.

Eschatology

What does all this mean for our eschatology?

Modern eschatological theories were formulated, in the first place, as a return to the Bible. They were trying to move away from the thoroughly unbiblical supernaturalism of treating the eschaton as a parallel, timeless, heavenly world that one enters into after death. That, we know, makes no sense of what Jesus and the prophets were saying about their *eschaton*.

What all the theories seem to have overlooked however, is that the Bible is not dealing with general religious truths. The message of the Bible is timebound, not in the sense that it reveals something about chronological times and dates, but in the sense that it records the quality of previous times in order to bring us face to face with God in our time.

Von Rad expressed this long ago apropos of the message of the prophets:

> It is all important not to read this message as if it consisted of timeless ideas, but to understand it as the particular word relevant to a particular hour in history, which therefore cannot be replaced by any other word. The prophetic word never tries to climb into the realm of general religious truth, but instead uses even the most suspect means to tie the listening partner down to their particular time and place in order to make them understand their own situation before God.

The Same God, the Same Revelation, the Same *Eschaton*: For the Israelites, the war against the Canaanites and the war against the Philistines was the same *kairos*—a time of war. For Jesus' contemporaries, the issue was whether a war against the Romans would be the same *kairos* or not the same challenge and the same hope.

With this in mind we can return to the *Kairos Document* and its implicit eschatology.

The *Kairos Document*

The *Kairos* theologians have drawn the conclusion that the present moment in South Africa is a *Kairos*, but they have not spelt out very clearly and in a truly prophetic manner why this particular moment should be regarded as a divine *kairos*. Reference is made to the conflict between oppressor and oppressed and to the division in the church, which claims the loyalty of both the oppressor and the oppressed. That indeed is a crisis and does raise some serious questions about the meaning of Christianity, but in and by itself it does not make our present time a *kairos*.

What is not explicit in the *Kairos Document*, although it is implied throughout the document, is that what we are now facing is our *eschaton*, what all the signs are now pointing to is that the day of liberation is near. Apartheid's days are numbered. In the near future this whole oppressive system is going to be utterly destroyed and a totally new, liberated and peaceful society will be built up in its place. The people are determined to do this and to do it soon and all the signs indicate that this drive towards liberation and peace through justice is now unstoppable. Of course it will be resisted, violently resisted, but it can no longer be stopped. This means that we must expect, unfortunately, more violence, more conflict and possibly more bloodshed before our society can be turned completely upside-down to become a land of justice and peace.

The Day of Reckoning is Near: In religious or theological terms, this is our *eschaton*. The day of Yahweh is at hand. The day of reckoning when God will put right what is wrong in our country is near. The terrifying seriousness of God's anger and love, of God's justice and mercy are about to descend upon us in a manner that might well make what the Old Testament prophets were talking about look like child's play. God is no less involved here in our present crisis and in the upheaval that is about to take place, than in the crisis and in the upheavals of the history of Israel.

A Time of Judgment and Salvation: That is what makes our present time in South Africa a truly prophetic *kairos*. A time of judgment and salvation. A time for real fear and trembling. A time when everything is at stake. A time for taking a clear stand. A time for tears and sadness that is nevertheless fraught with hope and joyful anticipation.

Time for Repentance and Radical Change: But it is also a time for us to act in the name of God, as the prophets did, to minimise the bloodshed. It is the sort of time when we should drop everything to proclaim from the rooftops that the day of reckoning is upon us and that the day of liberation has dawned. It is a time to appeal for immediate repentance and radical change; a time to call upon all in the world who can still hear the voice of God to do everything in their power, and at whatever cost to themselves, to hasten the downfall of the Apartheid regime and so bring the violence of oppression to a speedy end. Now is the time. God is near. That is the kind of eschatology that reverberates through the Bible. It has the same feel as the eschatology of the prophets and of Jesus himself.

Cardijn Studies: On the Church in the World of Today: Volume 4/2 2023

5
Integral Education

Presentation at the International Committees of The International Movement of Catholic Students (IMCS-Pax Romana) The International Young Catholic Students (IYCS) 20 August 2003

Introduction

The market rules almost everything in life today—including education. It is the market that demands that education focus primarily on scientific and technological knowledge. The result is that education today tends to be a matter of memorising rather than learning to think critically. Memorising produces parrots instead of people who are more aware and more fully human. And even when we study the social sciences or the humanities, we are expected to simply acquire more academic and intellectual information. We live in the age of information as if that were all we are capable of. An integral education would be an education that develops the whole person in the context of today's world. And it does this by developing not only the memory and the intellect, but also our consciousness as human beings.

My proposal in this talk will be that we try to think of education as the development of consciousness and to think of integral education as the development of an integral consciousness. Consciousness is not the same as knowledge or information. Consciousness involves the whole of one's being. It is an experience. While some people might make some subtle distinction between consciousness and awareness, I would say that consciousness is the same as awareness.

Social Consciousness

Consciousness is not a completely new word for our movements. We have always focused very strongly on social consciousness. Through the Review of Life or See-Judge-Act pedagogy we have developed in our members a deep social awareness. We have taught students to do social analysis, to search for the social causes of our problems, to ask questions about power relations in our societies and to be aware of the political and economic structures that govern the behavior of people.

Paulo Freire called this process 'conscientisation'. And our movements, both YCS and IMCS, have been in the forefront of this kind of education or pedagogy in the church.

Social consciousness is not the same as acquiring a great deal of information about different social theories or doing social research or studying sociology as an academic subject. That is very good and important and a valuable part of any integral education. But what our movements have done is something even more important. We have become socially aware, permanently conscious of the social dimension of all human life.

Today in our movements we are talking about change, not because we want to abandon our social consciousness (it is one of our greatest treasures), but because we want to expand our consciousness to include other forms of consciousness.

Global consciousness

Another form of consciousness that our movements have begun to develop, at least in some places, is what I would call global consciousness. It is an awareness of the vast diversity or pluralism that characterises our human world: different worldviews, cultures, religions and ways of thinking about life. Different people in different parts of the world see things in quite different ways and are motivated to do things for widely different reasons.

Men are becoming aware of how differently women see things. Older people are becoming aware of how vastly different the thinking of young people is today. Westerners are beginning to realise that the people of Africa and Asia experience life differently. Christians are now more conscious of the value of other religious faiths. Our postmodern society is learning to respect all people including those whom we see as mysteriously different from ourselves—the 'other' as they say.

Integral Education

Our movements have not always been sufficiently aware of the reality of these differences and especially our cultural and religious differences. We all need to develop a more global consciousness. No form of education today can be called integral if it does not develop in us a deep awareness of this pluralism.

Historical consciousness

While we often study history as an academic subject at school and at university, we don't always develop a good sense of history. Historical information is not the same as historical consciousness. An integral education would have to include not only a certain amount of historical information, but also an awareness of the vastly different experiences of people who lived in other times and places.

All thinking and experience are rooted in a particular historical context which influences the way people think and act. People in the past did not think the way we do, and we should not blame them for that. People in the future will have difficulty understanding how we thought in our day and why we did the things we did. What enables us to appreciate this is what we call an historical consciousness. Any form of education that deals with ideas in the abstract is misleading. An integral education will include a consciousness of the different historical contexts in which these ideas were conceived. Not because all truth is relative but because objective truth bas been conceived and formulated differently in different historical times.

Our movements have always emphasised the importance of memory. We try to remember and learn from the past history and experiences of our movements. But today when we are talking about change, we must also be conscious of the vast changes that have taken place in human consciousness in recent years. We live in a very different world today.

Evolutionary consciousness

One of the most dramatic changes in human consciousness in recent decades has been the result of modern discoveries about the nature of the universe in which we live. Darwin had made us aware of the fact that our human species, like all other living species, is the product of a long process of evolution. And then just as we were becoming used to thinking of ourselves as part of this biological evolution, Einstein and Hubble discovered that we are living in an unimaginably vast universe that is expanding all the time and has been growing and developing since the beginning of time, since what is now called the Big Bang or Original Flaring Forth. The whole universe bas been evolving or unfolding for 15 billion years. Starting with the simple atoms of hydrogen, all the other elements, molecules and minerals developed one from another in the great explosions that gave rise to billions of great galaxies and plant like our own sun and mother earth. And this unfolding or evolution is set to continue for who knows how long. And then there is quantum physics—the discovery that when you probe deeper and deeper into the particles in any atom to find out what they are made of. The scientists tell us that there is ultimately nothing there or rather nothing that our human minds can make sense of.

We live in a very mysterious universe that is moving forward on its own way quite independently of anything we may think or do, and we are simply part of it. Our human world with all its history and its problems is just a tiny speck in a grand miracle of development and growth that we cannot begin to control or even understand. As we think about change in our movements, in education, in the human world, we should remain ever conscious of that much, much bigger and broader context of the mysterious evolution or unfolding of the whole universe.

Ecological consciousness

Closely related to our consciousness of this evolving universe is another discovery of recent times—the discovery that we are in fact destroying our own environment, that is to say, planet, the planet to which we belong, the planet that gave birth to us and feeds us.

- We are polluting the rivers, the seas and the air.
- We are destroying the forests, washing the topsoil into the sea and creating more deserts by the day.
- Our chemicals are destroying the ozone layer that protects us from the ultra-violet rays of the sun.
- We are greedily depleting our natural resources, like oil and coal.
- In summary, what we are doing is upsetting the whole balance of nature in a way that can only be described as outrageously irresponsible.

Becoming aware of this is generally called 'ecological consciousness'. And here we can act. We can do something to save the earth. Ecological campaigns of one kind or another are springing up all over the world. Today there are as many eco-activists as activists working for social justice—if not more. In fact, the two go very well together as we discovered in South Africa last year (2002) with the World Summit on Sustainable Development. There is a very close relationship between economic justice and ecological justice because the principal reason why we continue to destroy the earth is money and profits.

While our movements cannot be involved in every cause in the world, we do need to include ecological concerns in any campaigns for an integral education. Education today without an ecological consciousness but as one integral and integrated consciousness of ourselves as individuals who can only exist as part of a structured society, a global human world, and as part of an evolving universe.

Consciousness of our inner selves

I had thought of calling this form of consciousness self-consciousness; but in English that has a pejorative meaning. It implies a kind of self-centeredness; What l want to draw your attention to is the importance of what is better know as self-knowledge. Psychology is concerned with this knowing of oneself and so is spirituality. All the best spiritual writers will tell you that you cannot know God unless you begin by getting to know yourself first. My argument will be that to be integral, education must include self- knowledge.

Many highly educated people have a vast amount of knowledge about everything and anything–except themselves. They are simply not aware of what is going on inside them, their unconscious motives, their inflated egos, their blind spots, their obsessions and compulsions.

Getting to know oneself is a lifelong pursuit, and a very important one, if we are going to avoid envies, jealousies, power struggles, hidden agendas and all the other confused motives that mess up the best laid plans and actions of our movements. Too often in the past we neglected this dimension. We neglected the needs of the individual person. Perhaps this was because so many Christians had focused exclusively on the individual in order to avoid any engagement with social realities. Our movements tended to compensate for this one-sided spirituality by putting the emphasis on social consciousness.

And sometimes we lost sight almost completely of the need for self-knowledge and a personal spirituality.

The consequences of this neglect of the personal and the self can be seen in the number of revolutions or social changes that have failed because of the greed and selfishness of some of those who inherited the power and authority. We obviously need both the social and the persona! Not just as two forms of consciousness, but as one integral and integrated consciousness of us individuals who can only exist as part of a structured society, a global human world, and as part of an evolving universe.

A fully integrated education must provide a person with the tools that will enable him or her to become more aware of themselves as persons, as unique persons, with their own personal and social history and their own particular skills and hang-ups.

An education that made us more aware of ourselves in this comprehensive context would be more integral than anything now had in our schools, our universities and even in our movements.

Consciousness of others as persons

The market treats people as economic objects, as consumers or producers or labor units, rather than as persons. Social consciousness too, has sometimes fallen into the trap of treating people as objects rather than subjects, as objects that fit into structures or power relations. The constant temptation is to treat workers, women, children, our rivals and anyone else as objects to be used or dealt with. Leaders of all kinds, including the leadership in the church and in our movements, tend to treat the people they lead as objects to be moved around or pushed aside in order to achieve the leader's aims and objectives. Even in education students are often seen as objects to be taught, while other people outside become objects of study.

But it is possible to become conscious of people as subjects rather than as objects, as persons rather than as things. It would be difficult to do it all the time with everyone we meet, but we know what it means to be in an '*I-Thous*' relationship with someone—a partner, a friend, a parent, a child.

Treating other people as persons is fundamental to Christian morality and spirituality. To love your neighbor as yourself is to treat your neighbor as another self, as a person like yourself and not as a mere thing to be used. Christian love means developing a consciousness of others as persons. One of the clearest signs of this consciousness is an eagerness to listen to others. That is the kind of consciousness that has to grow if we are ever to have a united, just, loving and peaceful world. An integral education will include some formation in this consciousness of others as persons.

God consciousness

Finally, there is a form of consciousness that is, in a sense, all-inclusive. It is the kind of spiritual or religious consciousness that, when it is genuine and mature, will arise out of all the other forms of consciousness. We call it GOD Consciousness.

God is not a person or a thing alongside of other persons or things. God is not one being amongst all the other beings in existence. God is in everything and beyond everything because God is the mystery in everything and behind everything. The emphasis in all theology today is on God as mystery. True belief in God is not about having an idea of God in one's head. It is about being conscious of God in the world, or better, being conscious of the presence of God as the mystery that gives rise to all things and sustains all things.

This is not as difficult and esoteric as it sounds. What it requires is the recognition or awareness of the limitations of our human knowledge. We can begin to experience the presence of God once we become conscious of the fact that there is much more out there, much more than we can ever know, a beyond that is totally mysterious and yet completely real.

We access this mystery through the human ability to wonder, to marvel, to stand in awe at the mysteriousness of it all.

Education often ignores or even destroys our sense of wonder. But today as we strive for an integral education, we will have to ensure that education includes the development of this sense of wonder at the mystery of it all, and therefore our consciousness of God's presence everywhere.

To that extent, an integral education will include something of a theological or faith education. If this is not provided in our schools and universities then it must come from the church and from our movements—otherwise our education will not be complete.

Cardijn Studies: On the Church in the World of Today: Volume 4/2 2023

6
A Spirituality of Action

International Training Session
JECI/MIEC
21 August 2003

International Committee Training Session

The Disciples of Jesus

Our movements have taught us to be disciples of Jesus of Nazareth. Our spirituality is based on following in the footsteps of Jesus, reliving his spirit in our lives today. We are his disciples. We learn from him.

We have a spirituality of action because Jesus was a man of action, that is, a person of action: He preached, he taught others, he educated them and challenged them.

- He healed the sick, physically and spiritually.
- He fed the hungry and gave strength to the poor.
- He exposed injustices by confronting hypocritical religious leaders, such as the Scribes and Pharisees.
- He was organising a movement or church with twelve apostles.
- It carried out symbolic actions of protest like the expulsion of the merchants and the moneylenders of the Temple.

Jesus was clearly a man of action and he taught others to do the same. He said that professing faith by saying, 'Lord, Lord', was not enough. We must do what he asks of us. Otherwise, it is like building on sand (Lk 6:46–49).

Action and reflection

Traditionally, in our movements, we distinguish between **actions** and **activities**. A good deed is based on careful reflection on an experience that demands a response, while an activity is the rest of the things one does without this formal process of reflection. Our method or pedagogy is described as Action–Reflection–Action or See–Judge–See. We do not act without having first reflected on the situation, without Seeing or Judging.

Another characteristic of our methodology is that we learn from our actions. The experience of doing often becomes an experience of the grace of God working with us, of hoping that things can change. Generally, we learn from our actions by reviewing them and carefully analysing what happened and why it happened in a certain way. Accordingly, the basis of a new action is our reflection on what we have done before.

We also try to judge the event or situation all the time in terms of our faith. Jesus taught us this too. His actions are the result of his reflections in prayer before God, of his contemplation:

- In the mornings he got up early to go to the mountains to pray before deciding to leave a certain place to go (Mk 1:35–38).
- Before choosing the twelve apostles, he spent the night in prayer and reflection (Lk 6:12–13).
- He spent forty days in the desert to reflect on his mission and his vocation.
- He prayed with great pain in the Garden of Gethsemane before deciding what to do since he was going to be arrested and crucified.

Thus, the opposite of a spirituality of action **is not** a spirituality of **contemplation**. We should not consider action and contemplation as different life options. It is true that some people as monks and sisters lead a life of pure contemplation and prayer. On the other hand, those who commit to a spirituality, their actions and reflections, their prayers and their contemplation inspire them to act with strength and with hope.

Escapist spirituality

The opposite of a spirituality of action is an escapist spirituality, that is to say, the type of individualism and egocentric spirituality which wants to leave the transformation of the world entirely to God.

This type of spirituality does not want to accept responsibility for change and does not even want to accept responsibility for thinking about what to do in relation to today's circumstances.

It becomes a spirituality of thoughtless obedience to their idea of the Will of God's and a blind obedience to all authorities, whether Church or State. This is the type of spiritualism that finds its security in authoritarianism. Fundamentalisms are based on such a spirituality.

Many people, among them some Christians, are afraid of freedom. They don't want to think for themselves in order to accept responsibility for his decisions or to take responsibility for what is happening in the world. They want others to make decisions for them and accept responsibility for their actions. Their spirituality is simply escapist.

Fundamentalists are slaves who choose to be fundamentalists because freedom is very dangerous and demanding. They will fight until death to remain slaves because they believe in a God who does not want them free.

Our spirituality of action is the opposite of this fundamentalist escapism. The Jesus who knows us and whom we follow exercised an astonishing freedom of spirit and also taught others to act and live in this way. 'Judge for yourselves', he said on one occasion, 'read the signs of the times'.

Jesus was able to act with great confidence and assurance precisely because he had absolute confidence in God. But Jesus' trust in God his Father was not a form of escapism. This trust did not lead him to avoid actions and decisions and leave them all to God. This confidence led him to act strongly and with unlimited hope and confidence.

In order to deepen our spirituality of action, we need to explore more of the awareness that made Jesus a man of action.

The consciousness of Jesus

Yesterday, in my presentation on integral education, I spoke of different types of consciousness, and I ended by speaking of the consciousness of Jesus.

Jesus had an unequaled and unprecedented awareness of God. He tested God in all things created and in all things that happened. In his life he experienced God as a Father, as his own Father. He trusted in God as one would trust in a loving father. He wanted to learn from God like a child wants to learn from his father. He imitated God as a son or a daughter would imitate his parents.

How do we know this? It is very difficult to get into the mind of Jesus, but his awareness of God as a loving Father is very evident when he talks about his Father saying **Abba**. Abba is an Aramaic word meaning father or dad. No one had ever dared to speak to God in such an intimate way. This word was transmitted to us in the language of Jesus, Aramaic, means that Jesus' use of this word was unique and striking.

For Jesus, God was not distant and distant. God was not a stern judge or an unsympathetic authority who asks for impossible things. For Jesus, God was a blind impersonal force to me. The great mysterious creator was his Abba. That's why we believe in Jesus as the Son of God.

However, this does not mean that Jesus thought he was the only one calling God Abba. He asks us to do it too. 'My Father is your Father', he said. 'And when you pray and say, "Our Father"'. God is very close to us too.

This was the secret of Jesus' own spirituality, his spirituality of action. This made him free and fearless. Since he felt completely loved by his Father, he didn't have to worry about what people thought of him or what they might do to him. He had plenty of courage and self-confidence.

Perhaps what our spirituality of action needs most now is a deeper awareness of God. Perhaps we need to explore private prayer as well as public and liturgical prayer. Perhaps, like Jesus, we must leave in order to be alone in silence, to be in touch with the great mystery behind all mysteries, the mystery that loves us like a father. Perhaps our reflections should include more elements of prayer and silent contemplation.

Others as people

I spoke yesterday about many other types of consciousness. Jesus was also an outstanding example of these other ways of awareness. Although in Jesus' time no one knew about the transformation of the universe or faced ecological problems, Jesus was very aware that creation was a manifestation of the glory and magnificence of God— whether the lilies of the field or the birds of the sky. Unfortunately, we cannot describe all these things about Jesus in this talk. For today's purpose, I will only talk about his awareness of other human beings as people more than objects, and the extraordinary compassion and love this gave him.

Jesus treated everyone he knew as unique people, each with his own particular story, his own feelings and desires, his sufferings and needs. He saw each person and reached out to all—especially those who were ignored and marginalised. He was immediately aware of them as people. The Gospels are full of stories that tell how Jesus approached people:

- He noticed the blind, the lame, and the invalids.
- He noticed the widow who put her last alms in the box for the poor.
- He took pity on Nain's widow, who is going to be poor because she has lost her only son.
- He approached the married Samaritan woman many times by the well.
- He treated children as people who deserved his attention in the same way as others.
- He saw Zacchaeus when he was sitting under the sycamore and he considered him a necessary man.

The acute awareness of individual people does not mean that he did not have a social conscience. The ideal future of which Jesus spoke was the 'Kingdom of God'. The 'Kingdom' is a social and structured reality, a community of people who care for each other and live together in a united society. The 'Kingdom' that Jesus preached and wanted was not a collection of objects but a society of people, who consider other people.

This type of consciousness of Jesus was **compassion**. The gospels continually tell us that Jesus 'dealt with compassion' with the sick, the lepers, the afflicted, the oppressed, the victims of oppression and domination. Compassion was a very strong emotion, and in the final analysis, this motivated him to act strongly and persistently.

Conclusion

Jesus' spirituality of action is based on two things: his unshakeable trust in God as his Father and his extraordinary compassion for people, that is, his awareness of God and his awareness of human beings as persons. We must learn this if we want to deepen our spirituality of action.

Many Christians today question spirituality. They seek inner peace, the meaning of life, hope. Our spirituality of action can give an answer to this need in ourselves and in others, since we follow Jesus by basing our actions in:

- serious reflection, using our methodology.
- in public and private prayer.
- in our search for the divine mystery, in whom we can trust as a loving.
- in the experience of compassion towards all your people, who are people like us.
- by regularly reviewing our actions in order to learn from them.

If we can develop a spirituality of action that is closer to this model, following in the footsteps of Jesus, I have no doubt that our movements will be re-energised. And if our movements are to be known by this type of spirituality of Jesus, we will become, I believe, **a sign of hope** in today's student environment.

And again, I am convinced that, with a solid commitment to Jesus and his spirituality of action, we will make an invaluable contribution to the Church in its current state of crisis, confusion and struggle. Our commitment to the Church must always be based on a more fundamental and primary commitment to Jesus.

Cardijn Studies: On the Church in the World of Today: Volume 4/2 2023

7
Biography of Albert Nolan OP
1934–2022

Born Denis James Harry Nolan in Cape Town on 2 September 1934, Albert Nolan OP was born to a family of South Africans of Irish descent, who lived in Gardens. He went to school at St Joseph's Marist Brothers in Rondebosch and after a period working for a bank, entered the Dominican Order in 1954, taking the name Albert.

Awarded the 'Order of Luthuli in Silver' by then President Thabo Mbeki in 2003 for his 'life-long dedication to the struggle for democracy, human rights and justice and for challenging the religious "dogma", especially the theological justification for apartheid', Nolan inspired a generation of Christian activists and theologians.

His dedication to the anti-Apartheid struggle saw him decline the prestigious role of Master of the Dominican Order to which he was elected in 1983, as it would have meant him being transferred to the Order's Rome headquarters. Instead, he convinced the Dominicans to allow him to remain in South Africa. At the height of the second State of Emergency in 1986, he was forced into hiding in order to escape from the notorious South African Security Police. Nolan was particularly vulnerable to arrest for steering the drafting process of the *Kairos Document* in mid-1985, which arose primarily from the work of grassroots theologians in Soweto and Johannesburg, but which he and Reverend Frank Chikane of the Institute for Contextual Theology (ICT) played a central role in editing. Described as a 'theology from below', the document critiqued the role of the churches in Apartheid South Africa, dismantled any theological justification for racism and totalitarianism and proposed instead a 'prophetic theology' akin to Liberation Theology.

From 1973–1980, he served as National Chaplain for the National Catholic Federation of Students (NCFS). In 1977, Nolan was instrumental in establishing Young Christian Students (YCS) in South Africa after he attended an International Movement of Catholic Students (IMCS) gathering in Lima, Peru, in 1975, where he was introduced to the See–Judge–Act method of social analysis and was inspired by Gustavo Gutiérrez, who later also became a Dominican and who is regarded as one of the pioneers of Liberation Theology. From 1977–1984, Nolan served as national chaplain of YCS, which affiliated itself to the United Democratic Front (UDF), initially formed in 1983 to oppose the Tricameral Parliament, but which also united more than 400 organisations across all sectors of society in the struggle for a 'non-racial, non-sexist and united South Africa'.

Nolan also played a brave role in the 'underground work' of the liberation movements, notably the African National Congress (ANC), offering his support to activists, especially those who became victims of the Apartheid regime's violent and repressive security police. He was part of a secret underground network that managed logistics, including the transportation and movement of activists, providing safe houses and a means of communication while in South Africa.

The full extent of his role in these networks was revealed by Horst Kleinschmidt in a tribute to Nolan on 20 October 2022. Kleinschmidt, who was himself banned, detained, and exiled by the Apartheid regime, disclosed that Nolan was part of a group of more than twenty operatives who smuggled communication out of South Africa to the then exiled ANC and returned with messages from Oliver Tambo and Thabo Mbeki to activists inside the country.

> I reveal today for the first time that Albert Nolan was known as operative A4 after Black Wednesday [19 October 1977, when Black Consciousness organisations were banned, editors arrested and opposition newspapers banned] and from 1981 onwards he was operative 42. The numbers '4' and '2' were scrambled into texts and figures—and the Security Branch never found the key to this messaging.

Kleinschmidt also revealed that the long-running operation involved the smuggling of letters, none of which were ever intercepted, as well as call-box to call-box communications that changed location each week and the swapping of money that made any tracing of bank records impossible.

Having been elected provincial of the Dominicans in Southern Africa in early 1976, Nolan relocated from Stellenbosch—where he had received his religious formation, and also served as university chaplain for several years up to the early 1970s—to Johannesburg. Poignantly, the move took place on June 16 1976, a date synonymous with the 'Soweto Uprising' which was violently suppressed and is today commemorated as Youth Day.

As provincial from 1976–1980, Nolan supported several of his priests—including Joe Falkiner OP, Benedict Mulder OP and Finbar Synnott OP—in their establishment of a simple-lifestyle community in a run-down building opposite the station on Central Avenue in Mayfair, a working-class suburb on the western edge of the Johannesburg central business district. He then made the bold decision to sell the provincial's house in the leafy suburb of Houghton, in the richer northern suburbs, and relocate to Mayfair himself, where CASA, NCFS, YCS and the Young Christian Workers (YCW) also set up their national offices. He served as provincial of the Dominican Order for two more terms, from 1980–1984 and from 2000–2004. Besides serving as provincial, Nolan played various other roles within his Order, including that of novice master and student master, which allowed him to continue to nurture and guide young people, as he had done for many years as a student chaplain.

A gifted biblical scholar and theologian, Nolan completed his doctorate in Rome in 1963–a period that coincided with the Second Vatican Council and which ushered in significant reforms across the Catholic Church. Having completed his thesis, Nolan decided it was 'too expensive' to have it published, a pre-requisite for being awarded the title of 'doctor' and thus, he never formally secured the title that he had duly earned. He was also initially denied the distinction of being awarded an honorary doctorate when the Holy See, without explanation, disallowed the University of Fribourg (Switzerland) from bestowing such in 1990, presumably owing to misgivings at the time about Liberation Theology. However, in the same year, as a sign of solidarity, the Jesuit-run Regis College of the University of Toronto granted him an honorary doctorate. The Dominican Order recognised his contribution as a theologian and preacher of the gospel when, in 2008, the Master of the Dominican Order promoted Nolan to a Master of Sacred Theology.

Outside of South Africa, Nolan became highly regarded for his 1976 best-selling book *Jesus before Christianity*, which has been translated into at least nine languages. The book was the product both of Nolan's deep knowledge of the Bible and his work in the student movement where he gave regular inputs on 'That Man Jesus' in student conferences. While in hiding in the late 1980s, Nolan went on to write *God in South Africa* (1988), which is the outcome of what he described as 'doing theology in a particular context', and *Jesus Today* (2007), which explores the spirituality of Jesus as a 'spirituality that leads to unity with God, ourselves, others, and the universe'. A collection of his talks, edited by one of his Dominican brothers, Fr Stan Muyebe OP, was published as *Hope in an Age of Despair* (2010).

Nolan, who was one of the first staff members of ICT in 1981, later became editor of the ecumenical *Challenge* magazine, widely circulated across all denominations and which offered a considered perspective on how Christians should respond to the struggle for democracy in South Africa before and after the democratic elections in 1994. Ecumenism was a theme throughout Nolan's life and was evident not only in his student ministry and at ICT but in his close relationship with leaders outside of the Catholic church, including Reverend Frank Chikane, Dr Beyers Naudé and Reverend Cedric Mayson. Despite his criticism of the Catholic Church, he also remained respected by the Catholic hierarchy for his biblical proficiency, his theological insight and his commitment to preaching the Gospel. He was, thus, regularly requested to deliver inputs and retreats, including to the Southern African Catholic Bishops' Conference, particularly when it was led by Archbishop Denis Hurley during the last decade of Apartheid.

Nolan was also a source of support to other religious in the Catholic church who took up an active role in the Struggle, notably Sr Bernard Ncube and Fr Smangaliso Mkhatshwa, who was detained several times and banned. Ncube was a member of the first democratic Parliament in 1994, chairing the portfolio committee on arts and culture, and in 2002 became mayor of the West Rand municipality. In 1996, Mkhatshwa became the Deputy Minister of Education, a post he held until 1999. He was elected to the ANC National Executive Committee in 1997 and in 2000 he became the Executive Mayor of the City of Tshwane.

In addition, Nolan taught at St Peter's Seminary, in Hammanskraal, in the late 1970's when a strong Black Consciousness focus was developed there, working particularly closely with Mkhatshwa and Buti Tlhagale in attempts to promote this voice in the church. Tlhagale is the current Archbishop of Johannesburg.

Albert Nolan died at the age of eighty-eight in the early hours of 17 October 2022. He died peacefully in his sleep under the care of the Dominican Sisters at Marian House in Boksburg, East Rand (Ekhuruleni) of Gauteng province of South Africa, where he had been for some years.

Published on Polity.org.za and written by Terence Creamer with input from Fr Mike Deeb OP, Fr Mark James OP and Prof Philippe Denis OP and with additions arising from tributes delivered by Fr Mark James and Horst Kleinschmidt on October 19 and 20 respectively.

Adapted from the website of the Order of Preachers, last accessed 1 April 2022.

Printed in the USA
CPSIA information can be obtained
at www.ICGtesting.com
LVHW040732201023
761199LV00005B/166